1. TAKE A BALL OF DOUGH

2. ROLL OUT THE DOUGH AND PLACE SOME FILLING ON IT.

3. CLOSE UP THE DOUGH AND FOLD THE EDGE.

4. YOUR EMPANADA IS READY TO BE COOKED!

EMPANADAS
ARGENTINIAN TURNOVERS!

ARGENTINIAN STREET FOOD

EMPANADAS, HELADOS & DULCE DE LECHE

ENRIQUE ZANONI AND GASTON STIVELMAHER

PHOTOGRAPHY **AKIKO IDA**
STYLING **SABRINA FAUDA-RÔLE**

MURDOCH BOOKS

CONTENTS

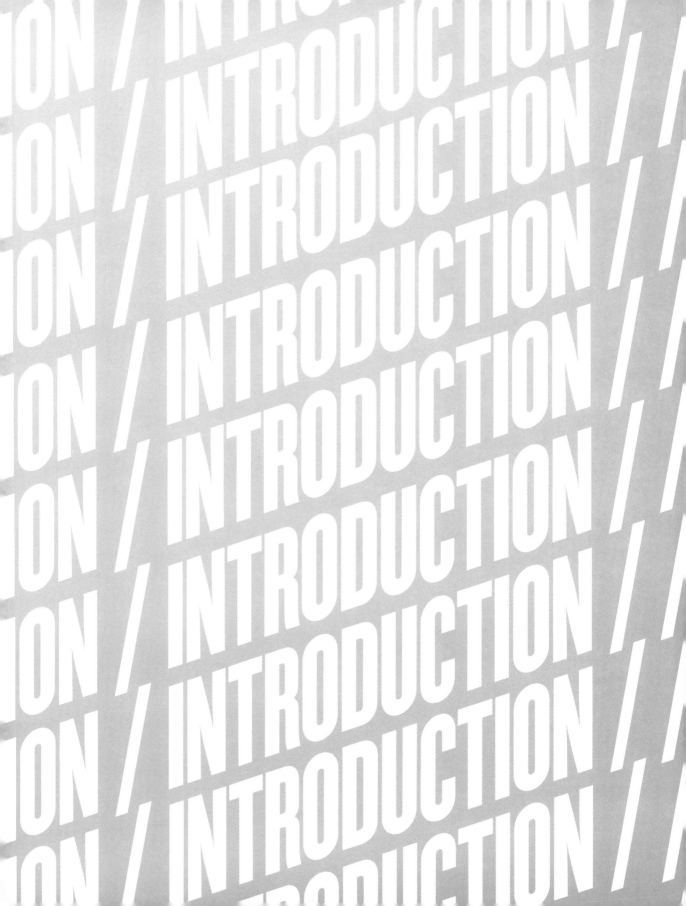

INTRODUCTION

A BOOK DEVOTED TO EMPANADAS AND HELADOS?

Some might think it's a strange idea to devote an entire book to stuffed pastries and ice cream. But these two very simple dishes are a crucial duo in Argentina. True gustatory pleasures, they are also synonymous with improvisation, celebration, friends and family. They're the elemental savoury/sweet double act that has a place on the tables of millions of South Americans every day. In Buenos Aires, as in all the big cities in Argentina, there are *casas de empanadas* and *heladerias* on every corner—almost as many as there are cafés or bakeries in France.

To introduce these items to lovers of good things, founder Enrique Zanoni and chef Gaston Stivelmaher inaugurated the Clasico Argentino concept in France in 2011.

Today Clasico Argentino has three restaurants in Paris and a food truck cruising the streets. Now here is a cookbook to pay tribute to the empanada, the *helado*, and the dulce de leche. In this book, Enrique Zanoni and Gaston Stivelmaher share their secrets so you can make these classics of Argentinian cuisine yourself.

¡ BUEN VIAJE Y BUEN PROVECHO !

CLASICO ARGENTINO IN PARIS

56 Rue de Saintonge 75003 PARIS
217 Rue du Faubourg Saint-Antoine 75011 PARIS
8 Rue du Pas de la Mule 75003 PARIS
EL CARRITO Food Truck concept
www.clasico-argentino.com
0 820 220 205

CLASICO ARGENTINO made its debut in France in Autumn 2011, in the heart of the Faubourg Saint-Antoine in the 11th Arrondissement. Two other locations opened shortly after (a second restaurant in the Marais and Clasico XS, a little shop in the 3rd Arrondissement). Argentinian flavours and culture take pride of place: the walls are the colours of the Albiceleste (the blue and white flag), the ceiling reproduces the pattern of the *cinta pampa*, an emblem of the country, and the furniture is wooden in the style of the traditional *tablitas* (large benches where you can enjoy empanadas). The 'grocery' section offers some typical Argentinian products: traditional *alfajores* (dulce de leche biscuits), great Argentinian wines such as Malbec or Torrontés, yerba mate tea, Quilmes or Sifon beer, inimitable sparkling water...

EL CARRITO Faithful to tradition, Clasico Argentino also has a mobile food cart that wanders through the streets of Paris. Called 'Carrito', it's a tribute to the Buenos Aires of the 1950s, when the *porteños*—residents of the port of Buenos Aires—would come to enjoy empanadas and ice cream from food vans set up on the banks of the Río de la Plata.

VINOS TINTOS

	VASO	BTTLA
MALBEC		
LA LINDA	4	19
LUIGI RESERVA	6	31
SAN PEDRO	8	34
MERLOT		
LUIGI RESERVA	6	32
ASSEMBLAGE		
RUTINI		36
GALA II		48

VINOS BLANCOS

	VASO	BTTLA
CHARDONNAY		
LA LINDA	4	19
TRAPICHE	4,5	20
TORRONTES	4	19
SAUVIGNON BLANC		
MARIFLOR		41

FERNET/RON COCA   7

CLASICO ARGENTINO
empanadas y helados

LAS EMPANADAS At Clasico Argentino, empanadas are high-end products equal to the most celebrated specialities of French cuisine. They are based on quality ingredients and cooked with passion according to tradition. The chef has reworked, diversified and improved the fillings: meat and spices, fish and herbs, unusual cheeses, gently cooked vegetables. Every day Clasico Argentino makes eight different fillings, and the chef offers a new one each month, depending on seasonal produce. You will find some of their secret combinations in this book.

CLASICO
VENTE A [
EMPANADAS
CARNE
QUESO Y JAMON
FUGAZETTA
POLLO
VERDURA
HUMITA
CHORIEMPA
ATUN
SALADE VERTE / MIXT
HELADOS:
FRESA
MELON
DULCE DE LECHE
CHOCOLATE
VAINILLA
MANGO
SAMBAYON
MARACUYA
BEBIDAS:
MALBEC

LOS HELADOS With deep roots in the collective memory, ice cream is to Argentinians what croissants or baguettes are to the French. To honour this much-enjoyed dessert, Clasico Argentino keeps to the traditional ice-cream making methods, selecting natural products, without preservatives or artificial flavours. Clasico Argentino offers ten flavours that vary according to the fruits in season.

LAS EMPANADAS

EMPANADAS

MEAT / VEGETABLE / CHEESE / SEAFOOD / SWEET

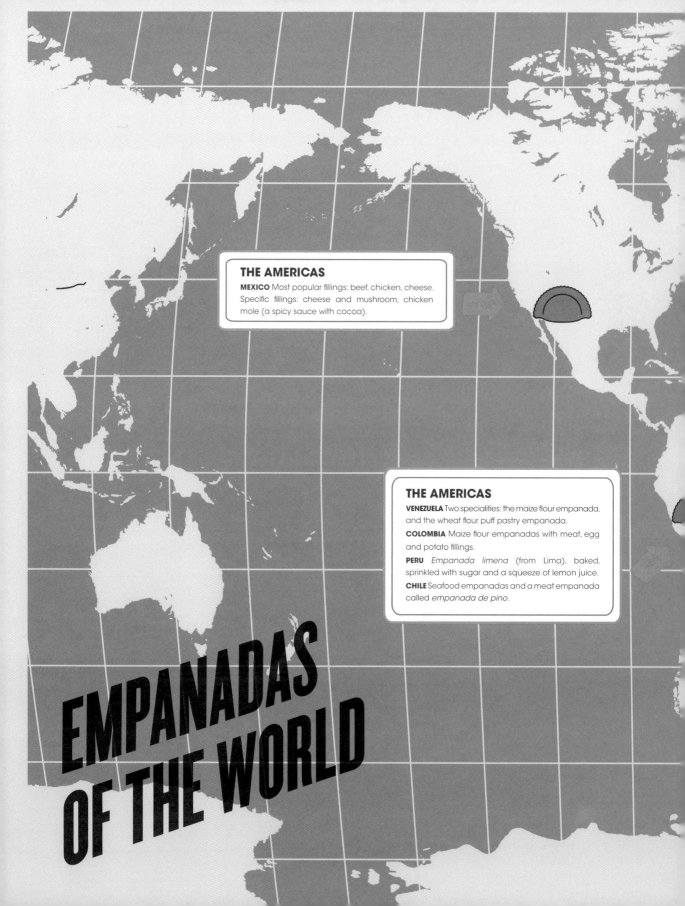

THE AMERICAS

MEXICO Most popular fillings: beef, chicken, cheese. Specific fillings: cheese and mushroom, chicken mole (a spicy sauce with cocoa).

THE AMERICAS

VENEZUELA Two specialities: the maize flour empanada, and the wheat flour puff pastry empanada.

COLOMBIA Maize flour empanadas with meat, egg and potato fillings.

PERU *Empanada limena* (from Lima), baked, sprinkled with sugar and a squeeze of lemon juice.

CHILE Seafood empanadas and a meat empanada called *empanada de pino*.

EMPANADAS OF THE WORLD

EUROPE

ITALY *Rustico leccese* (from Lecce in Puglia): puff pastry parcels with white sauce, mozzarella, tomatoes and black pepper. Another speciality, *panzerotto* or calzone made with fresh pizza dough.

FRANCE *Rissoles* (dating back to the Middle Ages): shortcrust pastry turnovers, sometimes crumbed, then fried or baked. Filling used in the Massif Central region: prunes.

RUSSIA

Piroshkis: world-famous stuffed buns filled with meat, rice, onion or mushrooms, usually served whole, or cut at the last minute.

NORTH AFRICA

Traditional dish: *briks*. Crisp pastry sheets filled with meat, eggs or potatoes. Spicy and highly aromatic fillings.

ASIA

JAPAN, CHINA AND KOREA Gyoza in Japan, *jiaozi* in China, *mandu* in Korea, steamed or fried.

MONGOLIA *Buuz* (steamed dumplings), *mantuun buuz* (filled with beef or mutton), *bansh* (meat dumplings in broth or soup).

INDONESIA Curry puffs: little fried pastries filled with chicken curry.

MANY COUNTRIES TODAY HAVE THEIR OWN 'EMPANADAS'. VARIATIONS EXIST THROUGHOUT THE WORLD, USING DIFFERENT KINDS OF DOUGH, FILLINGS AND COOKING METHODS. HERE ARE A FEW EXAMPLES.

EMPANADAS

THE ORIGIN OF EMPANADAS

It's hard to pin down the precise origin of the empanada, but it was probably inspired by a Spanish dish from the fifteenth century. Merchants and other nomads of the Iberian Peninsula would take on their travels an easy-to-carry bread that they filled with a variety of ingredients. Practical and simple to make, the empanada (from the verb *empanar*, literally 'to put in bread') has developed into a popular gastronomic item. From Russia to Italy via North Africa and France, the empanada has culinary equivalents in many countries. But France's *rissole* and Italy's calzone are nowhere near as famous as the empanada.

ARGENTINIAN STREET FOOD

In Buenos Aires, *casas de empanadas* are found throughout the city. It's deluxe 'fast-casual' food, gourmet takeaway, cooked using quality ingredients like Argentinian beef, local vegetables, etc. You take it with you and eat it wherever you want, preferably with your fingers!

AN EMPANADA FOR EVERY REGION

The empanada has an international reputation and the Argentinians have made it a jewel of their cuisine. From Salta to Buenos Aires, via Córdoba, Mendoza and Tucumán, the recipe varies. Olives, raisins, potatoes, eggs and other surprises, depending on the region, are added to beef, chicken, tuna, cheese, spinach or onions. Tucumán, which claims to be the province with the best empanadas, has even started a world empanada championship!

THE INGREDIENTS

**THE AMBITION OF CLASICO ARGENTINO WAS TO TURN A POPULAR
DISH INTO PART OF A BALANCED, GOURMET MEAL. THE INGREDIENTS
REMAIN VERY SIMPLE, AS IN THE TRADITIONAL VERSIONS, AND THE
EXPERTISE OF OUR ARGENTINIAN CHEF BRINGS THE FLAVOURS
OF ARGENTINA ALIVE IN HIGH-QUALITY EMPANADAS.**

FOR THE DOUGH

Gaston Stivelmaher prefers to use beef fat as is widely used in South America for the
dough, but butter or oil is used in these recipes as it is simpler for the domestic kitchen,
and also works well. Then only flour, water and salt are needed to make the dough.
While our chef also prefers to bake all his empanadas, leaving behind the deep-fried
style that's very common in South America, in this book we have included both baked
and deep-fried recipes.

FOR THE FILLING

Beef, corn, cheese, spinach, chicken and tuna are the most common empanada
fillings today. The choice of meat, vegetables, cheese and even butter is crucial, and
the quality of each ingredient can change everything.

With all the herbs, spices, vegetables or condiments you can add, and all the possible
combinations of meats, fish, vegetables, cheeses and various marinades, there are
endless empanadas to create. Each empanada is unique! You can create special
empanadas for different celebrations and festivals—mushroom empanadas in
autumn, for instance, or blue cheese empanadas for a surprise. Let yourself be inspired
by the season or the occasion to create original and delicious recipes.

THE SECRET OF THE CLASICO ARGENTINO FILLING

In the kitchens of Clasico Argentino, we rest the filling for two days in the refrigerator to
develop the flavours: they intensify over time. In these recipes, we recommend resting
the filling for 24 hours. This step is not compulsory, however, and the empanadas will
still work very well if you skip it.

THE RECIPES FOR THE DOUGH

THERE ARE TWO TYPES OF DOUGH, DEPENDING ON WHETHER THE EMPANADA IS BAKED OR FRIED. EACH RECIPE WILL MAKE 20 ROUNDS OF DOUGH, 14 CM (5½ INCHES) ACROSS. ALLOW ABOUT 30 MINUTES PREPARATION TIME AND 2 HOURS RESTING TIME.

CLASSIC DOUGH (FOR BAKING)

1. Cut 325 g (11½ oz) of unsalted butter into small cubes. Sift 1 kg (2 lb 4 oz/6⅔ cups) of plain (all-purpose) flour into a large bowl. Add 25 g (1 oz) of salt and the cubes of butter.

2. Rub the butter into the flour and salt with your hands until you have a sandy texture with no lumps.

3. Add 350 ml (12 fl oz) of water and combine with the flour mixture using your hands. Add a little more water if necessary. Knead the dough on a lightly floured work surface for 10–15 minutes.

4. Form into a ball. Wrap in plastic wrap and refrigerate for 2 hours.

PUFFED DOUGH (FOR FRYING)

1. Combine 1 kg (2 lb 4 oz/6⅔ cups) of plain (all-purpose) flour with 25 g (1 oz) of salt in a bowl.

2. Add 160 ml (5¼ fl oz) of sunflower oil and 350 ml (12 fl oz) of water, then mix with a wooden spoon.

3. Turn out onto a lightly floured work surface and knead for 10–15 minutes until smooth. Wrap in plastic wrap and refrigerate for 2 hours.

EL REPULGUE
THE TRADITIONAL DECORATION

'USE THE DECORATED EDGE AS A GUIDE TO THE FILLING HIDDEN INSIDE THE EMPANADAS.' WITH THIS INSTRUCTION, CLASICO ARGENTINO FOLLOWS THE ARGENTINIAN TRADITION OF THE 'REPULGUE'.

It's difficult, if not impossible, to translate the Spanish word *repulgue*. But this noun, which comes from the verb *repulgar*, meaning 'to hem', gives the empanada its character. The *repulgue* is the name of the decorative edging of the empanada. Traditionally, this edging is not just aesthetic, it also identifies the flavour of the empanada for the empanada-lover. Each empanada uses a specific pattern for each filling. Some have come to be associated with particular fillings over the years, so it's no surprise to find the same design throughout Argentina for beef, corn or chicken empanadas. Others, however, are specific to the particular *casa de empanada* or customised by the chefs who make them. Clasico Argentino has created eight *repulgue* of its own, while also using the more traditional patterns and adapting others (see page 26).

In Argentina, guessing the empanada filling has become a party game. Each person has to find their trio, quartet or quintet of empanadas based on their decoration. When someone accidentally eats someone else's empanada, they have to make it up by offering them one of their own. Since it's a common mistake, what someone eats often varies from what they ordered! To make it easier, at Clasico Argentino we slip in a sheet of paper showing the different *repulgue* inside the lunch or delivery box.

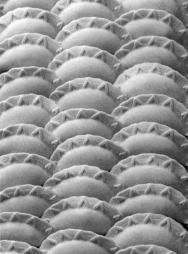

LAS EMPANADAS

THE FOLDING

WHILE MAKING THE EMPANADA DOUGH IS VERY EASY, YOU STILL NEED A BIT OF PRACTICE TO ACQUIRE THE TECHNIQUE OF FOLDING THEM.

1. Place the dough on a lightly floured work surface and roll it out to a thickness of 3 mm (⅛ inch). You may find it easier to roll half the dough at a time.

2. By hand, or with a cutter, cut out rounds 14 cm (5½ inches) across for the traditional version.

3. Using a 60 ml (2 fl oz/¼ cup) ice-cream scoop or measuring cup, form small balls of cooled filling and place one on each round of dough. Place the filling in the middle of each round, leaving about 1 cm (½ inch) between the filling and the edge of the dough.

4. Using your fingers, moisten the edge of the dough with a little water. Fold the round over onto itself into a half-moon shape. Pinch the edges with your fingers to seal the two edges of dough together.

5. To make the empanada edging, each pattern has its own technique. See page 26 for detailed instructions.

THE EDGING

AFTER SEALING THE EMPANADA, YOU CAN GIVE IT WHATEVER LOOK YOU LIKE, BASED ON THE TRADITIONAL DECORATIONS OR NOT. HERE ARE SOME REPULGUE USED BY CLASICO ARGENTINO.

CHORIEMPA (1) Place a sausage on the round of dough and fold the edges inward. Carefully wrap the sausage in the dough.

PASTELITO (2) Place a square of dough on the work surface. Place a portion of filling in the middle. Place a second square of dough on top, offsetting the corners relative to the first square, so you make an 8-pointed star. Pinch together the corners of the bottom square.

HUMITA (3) Once the empanada has been shaped into a half-moon, pinch the edge in five places to make a decoration with five points.

POLLO (4) Once the empanada has been shaped into a half-moon, seal the edges using a fork: mark the dough in five places to make a striped decoration.

CORDERO (5) Once the empanada has been shaped into a half-moon, make waves in the edge with your fingers.

JAMON Y QUESO (6) Once the empanada has been shaped into a half-moon and the edges are well sealed, bring the two points towards each other and join them together.

PUERRO (7) Once the empanada has been shaped into a half-moon and the edges are well sealed, gather the two points together and join them while keeping the edging quite flat, so your empanada is almost circular.

CARNE (8) Once the empanada has been shaped into a half-moon and the edges are well sealed, fold the edges over themselves 13 consecutive times, from one end to the other (see illustrations below).

The 'carne' decoration is the most classic edging, the 'pollo' one is the easiest to do.

You will encounter still more decorations at Clasico Argentino. These are the most common ones.

SAUCES

Here are three traditional Argentinian recipes to serve with the empanadas.

SALSA CAYENA

PREPARATION TIME:
10 MINUTES

MAKES 375 ML
(13 FL OZ/1½ CUPS)

INGREDIENTS
2 tomatoes
1 small onion
1 garlic clove

1 fresh small red chilli,
  finely diced
1 tablespoon aji molido
  (see glossary) (optional)

3 teaspoons cayenne
  pepper
60 ml (2 fl oz/¼ cup) olive oil
salt, black pepper

Cut the tomatoes in half and grate the flesh, discarding the skin. Chop the onion and garlic. Mix together, then add the chilli, aji molido, if using, cayenne pepper, oil, salt and pepper. Store in an airtight container.

GREEN CHIMICHURRI

PREPARATION TIME:
15 MINUTES

MAKES 875 ML
(30 FL OZ/3½ CUPS)

BASE INGREDIENTS
6 spring onions
  (scallions), sliced
200 ml (7 fl oz) white
  wine vinegar
300 ml (10½ fl oz) olive oil
1 fresh bay leaf
2 garlic cloves, unpeeled
salt, black pepper

HERBS
90 g (3¼ oz/1 bunch)
  fresh oregano
2 rosemary stalks
150 g (5½ oz/1 bunch)
  flat-leaf (Italian) parsley
80 g (2¾ oz/1 bunch) mint
90 g (3¼ oz/1 bunch)
  coriander (cilantro) leaves

1 bunch tarragon
1 bunch chervil
20 g (¾ oz/1 bunch) thyme

Finely chop all the herbs and mix them in a large bowl. Add the spring onion. (Alternatively, chop the herbs and spring onion in a food processor.) Stir in the vinegar, oil, bay leaf and bruised garlic cloves. Season with salt and pepper and store in an airtight jar. This sauce will keep in the refrigerator for about 10 days. Remove the bay leaf and garlic before serving.

CLASICO ARGENTINO CHIMICHURRI

PREPARATION TIME:
15 MINUTES

MAKES 1.25 LITRES
(44 FL OZ/5 CUPS)

BASE INGREDIENTS
2 white onions
2 red capsicums (peppers)
1 fresh small red chilli
150 g (5½ oz/1 bunch)
  flat-leaf (Italian) parsley
90 g (3¼ oz/1 bunch)
  coriander (cilantro)

250 ml (9 fl oz/1 cup)
  red wine vinegar or
  sherry vinegar
300 ml (10½ fl oz)
  sunflower oil
1 fresh bay leaf
1 cinnamon stick
2 garlic cloves, unpeeled
salt, black pepper

DRY SPICES
2 tablespoons dried
  oregano
2 tablespoons aji molido
  (see glossary) or
  1 tablespoon chilli flakes
3 teaspoons ground cumin
2 tablespoons paprika

Combine the dry spices in a large bowl and pour over 100 ml (3½ fl oz) of boiling water to bring out their flavours. Allow to cool. Finely dice the onion, capsicum and chilli. Chop the parsley and coriander leaves. Mix the vegetables and herbs into the spice mixture. (Alternatively chop all the vegetables and herbs in a food processor, then add the spice mixture.) Add the vinegar, oil, bay leaf, cinnamon stick and the bruised garlic cloves, stirring to combine. Season with salt and pepper and spoon into an airtight jar. The sauce will keep in the refrigerator for about 10 days. Remove the garlic before serving.

CLASICO ARGENTINO

PREPARATION TIME:
40 MINUTES

RESTING TIME (OPTIONAL):
24 HOURS

COOKING TIME:
50 MINUTES

MAKES 20 EMPANADAS

DOUGH
1 quantity of classic
   dough (see page 20)

FILLING
2 onions, sliced
1 red capsicum
   (pepper), sliced
sunflower oil
salt, black pepper

500 g (1 lb 2 oz) minced
   (ground) beef
1 tablespoon aji molido
   (see note below) or
2 teaspoons of chilli flakes
1½ tablespoons ground
   cumin
3 teaspoons paprika
3 teaspoons ground
   cinnamon

6 spring onions (scallions),
   green part only, chopped

GLAZE
3 egg yolks, beaten

FILLING

Sauté the onion and capsicum in a saucepan with a little oil over low heat for
10 minutes. Season with salt and pepper. Remove the vegetables from the saucepan
and set aside.

To the same saucepan, add a little more oil and sauté the meat over high heat. Once
the meat has browned, reduce heat to low and add the onion and capsicum. Continue
cooking for about 15 minutes, stirring from time to time. Stir in the aji molido, if using,
cumin, paprika and cinnamon and mix well.

Let the filling rest for 24 hours in the refrigerator, if possible, for a more intense flavour.
Stir the spring onion into the mixture before assembling the empanadas.

ASSEMBLY

Preheat the oven to 190°C (375°F/Gas 5). Sprinkle a little flour on the work surface.
Roll out the dough to a thickness of 3 mm (⅛ inch), and cut out circles with a 14 cm
(5½ inch) cutter. Using a 60 ml (2 fl oz/¼ cup) ice-cream scoop or measuring cup, form
small balls of filling and place one on each round of dough. Lightly moisten the edge of
the dough with a little water and fold over into a half-moon shape. Seal the edges and
give them the 'carne' decoration (see page 26) or an edging of your choice. Set aside
in the refrigerator if not cooking immediately.

COOKING

Arrange the empanadas on a baking tray lined with baking paper. Brush with egg yolk
and bake for 20 minutes, or until golden and cooked. Allow them to cool for a few
minutes before serving.

AJI MOLIDO

A very common condiment in Argentinian cuisine, made from dried capsicum
flakes. It can be found in Argentinian grocery stores.

SALTEÑA

PREPARATION TIME:
40 MINUTES

RESTING TIME (OPTIONAL):
24 HOURS

COOKING TIME:
55 MINUTES

MAKES 20 EMPANADAS

DOUGH
1 quantity of puffed
   dough (see page 20)

FILLING
500 g (1 lb 2 oz) rump steak
2 potatoes, about 300 g
   (10½ oz) in total
2 onions, sliced
olive oil
1½ tablespoons ground
   cumin
1½ tablespoons chilli
   powder
salt, black pepper
6 hard-boiled eggs,
   chopped
6 spring onions (scallions),
   green part only, chopped

FOR FRYING
1.5 litres (52 fl oz/6 cups)
   sunflower oil

FILLING

Cut the steak into small cubes. Bring a large saucepan of water to the boil and blanch the meat for 3 minutes. Drain and set aside.

Peel the potatoes, cut them into small cubes and boil in salted water for about 8 minutes. They need to be cooked but still firm. Drain and set aside.

Sauté the onion in a frying pan with a little oil over low heat for 15 minutes. Add the meat and cook for a further 5 minutes. Add the cumin, chilli powder, salt and pepper.

Let the filling rest for 24 hours in the refrigerator, if possible, for a more intense flavour.

ASSEMBLY

Sprinkle a little flour on the work surface. Roll out the dough to a thickness of 3 mm (⅛ inch) and cut out circles with a 14 cm (5½ inch) cutter. Using a 60 ml (2 fl oz/¼ cup) ice-cream scoop or measuring cup, form small balls of filling and place one on each round of dough. Before closing the empanadas, add the egg and spring onion. Lightly moisten the edge of the dough with a little water and fold over into a half-moon shape. Seal the edges and give them the 'carne' decoration (see page 26) or an edging of your choice. Set aside in the refrigerator if not cooking immediately.

COOKING

In a saucepan or deep-fryer, heat the oil for frying to 180°C (350°F), or until a cube of bread dropped into the oil turns golden brown in 15 seconds. Add a few empanadas to the oil, and fry for 5 minutes, or until browned. Remove from the oil and drain on paper towels. Repeat this process with the remaining empanadas. Allow them to cool for a few minutes before serving.

REGIONAL RECIPE

This recipe comes from the north of Argentina, from the province of Salta.

CORDOBESA

PREPARATION TIME:
40 MINUTES

RESTING TIME (OPTIONAL):
24 HOURS

COOKING TIME:
50 MINUTES

MAKES 20 EMPANADAS

DOUGH
1 quantity of puffed
dough (see page 20)

FILLING
600 g (1 lb 5 oz) beef
eye fillet
2 onions, diced
1 red capsicum (pepper),
diced
olive oil

3 tomatoes, peeled, seeded
and chopped
salt, black pepper
1½ tablespoons ground
cumin
3 teaspoons sugar
3 tablespoons raisins
3 tablespoons pitted green
olives, sliced
6 spring onions (scallions),
green part only, chopped

FOR FRYING
1.5 litres (52 fl oz/6 cups)
sunflower oil

FILLING

Cut the meat into thin strips. Bring a saucepan of water to the boil and blanch for
3 minutes. Drain and set aside.

Sauté the onion and capsicum in a flameproof casserole dish with a little oil for
5 minutes, or until softened. Add the tomato and cook for 10 minutes over medium heat.
Add the meat and cook for a further 5 minutes. Season with salt, pepper, cumin and
sugar. Add the raisins and olives.

Let the filling rest for 24 hours in the refrigerator, if possible, for a more intense flavour.
Stir the spring onion into the mixture before assembling the empanadas.

ASSEMBLY

Sprinkle a little flour on the work surface. Roll out the dough to a thickness of 3 mm
(⅛ inch) and cut out circles with a 14 cm (5½ inch) cutter. Using a 60 ml (2 fl oz/¼ cup)
ice-cream scoop or measuring cup, form small balls of filling and place one on each
round of dough. Lightly moisten the edge of the dough with a little water and fold over
into a half-moon shape. Seal the edges and give them the 'carne' decoration (see
page 26) or an edging of your choice. Set aside in the refrigerator if not cooking
immediately.

COOKING

In a saucepan or deep-fryer, heat the oil for frying to 180°C (350°F), or until a cube of
bread dropped into the oil turns golden brown in 15 seconds. Add a few empanadas to
the oil, and fry for 5 minutes, or until browned. Remove from the oil and drain on paper
towels. Repeat this process with the remaining empanadas. Allow them to cool for a few
minutes before serving.

REGIONAL RECIPE
This recipe comes from the north of Argentina, from the province of Córdoba.

TUCUMANA

 PREPARATION TIME:
40 MINUTES

 RESTING TIME (OPTIONAL):
24 HOURS

 COOKING TIME:
1 HOUR 15 MINUTES

MAKES 20 EMPANADAS

DOUGH
1 quantity of puffed
dough (see page 20)

FILLING
500 g (1 lb 2 oz) flank steak
2 onions, sliced
olive oil

1½ tablespoons ground
cumin
1½ tablespoons chilli
powder
salt, black pepper
6 hard-boiled eggs,
chopped
6 spring onions (scallions),
green part only, chopped

FOR FRYING
1.5 litres (52 fl oz/6 cups)
sunflower oil

FILLING

Poach the meat in a large saucepan of salted water for 35 minutes over low heat.
Cut into small cubes.

Sauté the onion in a frying pan with a little oil over low heat for 10 minutes. Add the meat
and continue cooking for 5 minutes. Season with cumin, chilli powder, salt and pepper.
Mix in the egg and spring onion.

Let the filling rest for 24 hours in the refrigerator, if possible, for a more intense flavour.

ASSEMBLY

Sprinkle a little flour on the work surface. Roll out the dough to a thickness of 3 mm
(⅛ inch), and cut out circles with a 14 cm (5½ inch) cutter. Using a 60 ml (2 fl oz/¼ cup)
ice-cream scoop or measuring cup, form small balls of filling and place one on each
round of dough. Lightly moisten the edge of the dough with a little water and fold over
into a half-moon shape. Seal the edges and give them the 'carne' decoration (see
page 26) or an edging of your choice. Set aside in the refrigerator if not cooking
immediately.

COOKING

In a saucepan or deep-fryer, heat the oil for frying to 180°C (350°F), or until a cube of
bread dropped into the oil turns golden brown in 15 seconds. Add a few empanadas
to the oil, and fry for 5 minutes, or until browned. Remove from the oil and drain on paper
towels. Repeat this process with the remaining empanadas. Allow them to cool for a few
minutes before serving.

REGIONAL RECIPE

This recipe comes from the north of Argentina, from the province of Tucumán. It
uses beef fat (available from the butcher), like the traditional empanada, which
gives it a unique flavour. Try substituting melted beef fat for the oil both in the
dough recipe and for frying.

CARNE PICANTE

PREPARATION TIME:
40 MINUTES

RESTING TIME (OPTIONAL):
24 HOURS

COOKING TIME:
50 MINUTES

MAKES 20 EMPANADAS

DOUGH
1 quantity of classic
  dough (see page 20)

FILLING
1 large onion, sliced
1 red capsicum
  (pepper), sliced
olive oil

salt, black pepper
500 g (1 lb 2 oz) minced
  (ground) beef (20% fat)
4 fresh small red
  chillies, chopped
1 tablespoon aji molido
  (see glossary) (optional)
1½ tablespoons ground
  cumin

3 teaspoons chilli powder
6 spring onions (scallions),
  green part only, chopped

GLAZE
3 egg yolks, beaten

FILLING

Sauté the onion and capsicum in a saucepan with a little oil over low heat for
10 minutes. Season with salt and pepper. Remove the vegetables from the saucepan
and set aside.

To the same saucepan, add a little more oil and brown the meat over high heat for a
few minutes. Add the onion, capsicum and chilli and cook over low heat for 15 minutes.
Add the aji molido, if using, cumin and chilli powder and mix to combine.

Let the filling rest for 24 hours in the refrigerator, if possible, for a more intense flavour.
Stir the spring onion into the mixture before assembling the empanadas.

ASSEMBLY

Preheat the oven to 190°C (375°F/Gas 5). Sprinkle a little flour on the work surface.
Roll out the dough to a thickness of 3 mm (⅛ inch), and cut out circles with a 14 cm
(5½ inch) cutter. Using a 60 ml (2 fl oz/¼ cup) ice-cream scoop or measuring cup, form
small balls of filling and place one on each round of dough. Lightly moisten the edge of
the dough with a little water, and fold over into a half-moon shape. Seal the edges and
give them the 'carne' decoration (see page 26) or an edging of your choice. Set aside
in the refrigerator if not cooking immediately.

COOKING

Arrange the empanadas on a baking tray lined with baking paper. Brush with egg yolk
and bake for 20 minutes, or until golden and cooked. Allow them to cool for a few
minutes before serving.

CHORIEMPA

PREPARATION TIME:
20 MINUTES

COOKING TIME:
40 MINUTES

MAKES 20 EMPANADAS

DOUGH
1 quantity of classic
  dough (see page 20)

FILLING
20 small pork sausages,
  8–9 cm (3¼–3½ inches)
olive oil

GLAZE
3 egg yolks, beaten

TO SERVE
Clasico Argentino
  chimichurri (see page 28)

FILLING

Brown the sausages in a hot frying pan with a little oil over high heat. Cover with water and cook for 15 minutes over medium heat until cooked through. Drain and allow to cool.

ASSEMBLY

Preheat the oven to 190°C (375°F/Gas 5). Sprinkle a little flour on the work surface. Roll out the dough to a thickness of 3 mm (⅛ inch), and cut out circles with a 14 cm (5½ inch) cutter. Place a sausage on each circle of dough and fold the edges inward. Carefully roll each sausage in the dough. This is the 'choriempa' fold (see page 26). Set aside in the refrigerator if not cooking immediately.

COOKING

Arrange the empanadas on a baking tray lined with baking paper. Use a knife to cut a few slashes on top of each one. Brush with egg yolk and bake for 20 minutes, or until golden and cooked. Allow them to cool for a few minutes before serving with the chimichurri sauce.

CHORIPAN

This recipe is a variation of a classic dish called 'choripan'.
The original version is a sausage sandwich, which we rework at Clasico Argentino
by using empanada dough.

SWEET & SOUR CHICKEN

PREPARATION TIME:
30 MINUTES

RESTING TIME (OPTIONAL):
3 HOURS

COOKING TIME:
45 MINUTES

MAKES 20 EMPANADAS

DOUGH
1 quantity of puffed
  dough (see page 20)

FILLING
500 g (1 lb 2 oz)
  chicken breast fillet
olive oil
1 tablespoon sugar
1 large onion, chopped
1 yellow capsicum
  (pepper), chopped
1 garlic clove, chopped
2 tablespoons tomato paste
  (concentrated purée)
100 ml (3½ fl oz) white
  wine vinegar
200 ml (7 fl oz) chicken
  stock
1 pinch of saffron threads
salt, black pepper
25 g (1 oz/1 bunch)
  chives, chopped

FOR FRYING
1.5 litres (52 fl oz/6 cups)
  sunflower oil

FILLING

Cut the chicken into small cubes and brown in a saucepan with a little oil over high heat until golden. Sprinkle with the sugar and let it caramelise for 2 minutes. Add the onion, capsicum and garlic and cook for 3 minutes over low heat. Add the tomato paste, vinegar, stock and saffron, and continue cooking for 15 minutes, or until the liquid has reduced. Season with salt and pepper. Add the chives. Cool to room temperature and set aside in the refrigerator for 3 hours, if possible.

ASSEMBLY

Sprinkle a little flour on the work surface. Roll out the dough to a thickness of 3 mm (⅛ inch) and cut out circles with a 14 cm (5½ inch) cutter. Using a 60 ml (2 fl oz/¼ cup) ice-cream scoop or measuring cup, place a portion of filling on each round. Lightly moisten the edge of the dough with a little water and fold over into a half-moon shape. Seal the edges and give them the 'pollo' decoration (see page 26) or an edging of your choice. Set aside in the refrigerator if not cooking immediately.

COOKING

In a saucepan or deep-fryer, heat the oil for frying to 180°C (350°F), or until a cube of bread dropped into the oil turns golden brown in 15 seconds. Add a few empanadas to the oil, and fry for 5 minutes, or until brown. Remove from the oil and drain on paper towels. Repeat this process with the remaining empanadas. Allow them to cool for a few minutes before serving.

CHICKEN & CORIANDER

PREPARATION TIME:
30 MINUTES

RESTING TIME (OPTIONAL):
24 HOURS

COOKING TIME:
45 MINUTES

MAKES 20 EMPANADAS

DOUGH
1 quantity of puffed dough (see page 20)

FILLING
500 g (1 lb 2 oz) chicken breast fillet
sunflower oil
1 onion, sliced
1 yellow capsicum (pepper), sliced
1½ tablespoons finely grated fresh ginger
3 garlic cloves, finely chopped
2 tablespoons tomato paste (concentrated purée)
a little chicken stock or water
3 teaspoons ground cumin
3 teaspoons dried oregano
90 g (3¼ oz/1 bunch) coriander (cilantro) leaves, chopped
salt, black pepper

FOR FRYING
1.5 litres (52 fl oz/6 cups) sunflower oil

FILLING

Cut the chicken into small pieces. Brown the chicken in a heavy-based saucepan with a little oil over medium heat. Add the onion, capsicum, ginger and garlic to the pan. Stir in the tomato paste and cook for 10 minutes over low heat. Add a little stock if it starts to catch on the base of the pan.

Cool the filling and chop in a food processor. Add the cumin, oregano and coriander. Season with salt and pepper.

Let the filling rest for 24 hours in the refrigerator, if possible, for a more intense flavour.

ASSEMBLY

Sprinkle a little flour on the work surface. Roll out the dough to a thickness of 3 mm (⅛ inch) and cut out circles with a 14 cm (5½ inch) cutter. Using a 60 ml (2 fl oz/¼ cup) ice-cream scoop or measuring cup, form small balls of filling and place one on each round of dough. Lightly moisten the edge of the dough with a little water and fold over into a half-moon shape. Seal the edges and give them the 'pollo' decoration (see page 26) or an edging of your choice. Set aside in the refrigerator if not cooking immediately.

COOKING

In a saucepan or deep-fryer, heat the oil for frying to 180°C (350°F), or until a cube of bread dropped into the oil turns golden brown in 15 seconds. Add a few empanadas to the oil, and fry for 5 minutes, or until they brown. Remove from the oil and drain on paper towels. Repeat this process with the remaining empanadas. Allow them to cool for a few minutes before serving.

LAMB
PATAGONIA STYLE

PREPARATION TIME:
40 MINUTES

RESTING TIME:
2 HOURS

COOKING TIME:
55 MINUTES

MAKES 20 EMPANADAS

DOUGH
1 quantity of puffed dough
(see page 20)

FILLING
600 g (1 lb 5 oz)
   boned lamb leg
olive oil
1 tablespoon honey
300 ml (10½ fl oz) red wine

1 large onion, sliced
1 red capsicum
   (pepper), sliced
2 garlic cloves, sliced
1 pinch of merkén (see note
   below) or smoked paprika
salt, black pepper
3 teaspoons chopped
   rosemary
3 teaspoons thyme leaves

3 teaspoons chopped
   tarragon
1 handful of mint leaves,
   chopped

FOR FRYING
1.5 litres (52 fl oz/6 cups)
   sunflower oil

FILLING

Cut the lamb into 1 cm (½ inch) cubes. Brown over high heat in a saucepan with a little oil for a few minutes. Add the honey and let the meat caramelise for 2 minutes. Pour in the red wine and bring to the boil, stirring, for 30 seconds to deglaze the pan, then lower heat and reduce the liquid for 5 minutes. Stir in the onion, capsicum, garlic, merkén, salt and pepper. Lower heat again and continue cooking for 20 minutes, or until the wine has evaporated. Add the rosemary, thyme, tarragon and mint.

Let the mixture cool, then refrigerate for 2 hours.

ASSEMBLY

Sprinkle a little flour on the work surface. Roll out the dough to a thickness of 3 mm (⅛ inch) and cut out circles with a 14 cm (5½ inch) cutter. Using a 60 ml (2 fl oz/¼ cup) ice-cream scoop or measuring cup, form small balls of filling and place one on each round of dough. Lightly moisten the edge of the dough with a little water and fold over into a half-moon shape. Seal the edges and give them the 'cordero' decoration (see page 26) or an edging of your choice. Set aside in the refrigerator if not cooking immediately.

COOKING

In a saucepan or deep-fryer, heat the oil for frying to 180°C (350°F), or until a cube of bread dropped into the oil turns golden brown in 15 seconds. Add a few empanadas to the oil, and fry for 5 minutes, or until they brown. Remove from the oil and drain on paper towels. Repeat this process with the remaining empanadas. Allow them to cool for a few minutes before serving.

MERKÉN

Merkén is a spice that's widely used in Patagonia and Chile. It's a chilli powder with a strong, smoky flavour. It can be found in grocery stores all over the world. If you can't find it, use smoked paprika instead.

GALA
DUCK CONFIT & FOIE GRAS

PREPARATION TIME:
30 MINUTES

COOKING TIME:
3 HOURS 45 MINUTES

MAKES 20 EMPANADAS

DOUGH
1 quantity of classic
    dough (see page 20)

FILLING
1 kg (2 lb 4 oz) duck
    or goose fat
6 duck leg quarters
5 star anise
1 tablespoon coriander
    seeds
1 cinnamon stick
1 tablespoon black
    peppercorns
500 g (1 lb 2 oz) foie gras
salt, black pepper
a few leaves of flat-leaf
    (Italian) parsley, chopped
a few leaves of tarragon,
    chopped
finely grated zest and
    juice of 1 orange

GLAZE
3 egg yolks, beaten

TO SERVE
sugar for sprinkling

FILLING

Melt the fat in a large saucepan that's large enough to hold the duck in one layer. When melted, add the duck, star anise, coriander seeds, cinnamon stick and peppercorns. Cook over low heat for 3 hours. Take out the duck. When cool remove the meat and shred finely.

Cut the foie gras into slices 2 cm (¾ inch) thick. In a hot frying pan without any fat, brown the slices for 3 minutes on each side. Season with salt and pepper. Remove them to a tray lined with paper towels, then cut into small cubes.

Combine the foie gras with the shredded duck confit, parsley and tarragon. Add the orange zest and juice.

ASSEMBLY

Preheat the oven to 190°C (375°F/Gas 5). Sprinkle a little flour on the work surface. Roll out the dough to a thickness of 3 mm (⅛ inch), and cut out circles with a 14 cm (5½ inch) cutter. Using a 60 ml (2 fl oz/¼ cup) ice-cream scoop or measuring cup, form small balls of filling and place one on each round of dough. Lightly moisten the edge of the dough with a little water and fold over into a half-moon shape. Seal the edges and give them the 'carne' decoration (see page 26) or an edging of your choice. Set aside in the refrigerator if not cooking immediately.

COOKING

Arrange the empanadas on a baking tray lined with baking paper. Brush them with egg yolk and bake for 20 minutes, or until golden and cooked. Remove the tray from the oven and sprinkle the empanadas with sugar. Allow them to cool for a few minutes before serving.

SPINACH & CHEESE

PREPARATION TIME:
30 MINUTES

COOKING TIME:
40 MINUTES

MAKES 20 EMPANADAS

DOUGH
1 quantity of classic
dough (see page 20)

BÉCHAMEL
70 g (2½ oz) unsalted butter
70 g (2½ oz) plain
(all-purpose) flour
700 ml (24 fl oz) milk
salt, black pepper

1 pinch of freshly grated
nutmeg

FILLING
700 g (1 lb 9 oz) baby
spinach
olive oil
salt, black pepper
200 g (7 oz) mozzarella
or feta cheese, diced

100 g (3½ oz) parmesan
or Grana Padano
cheese, grated

GLAZE
3 egg yolks, beaten

BÉCHAMEL

Melt the butter in a saucepan over low heat. Stir in the flour and mix with a wooden spoon. Cook, stirring, for 4 minutes, then add the milk, stirring constantly to avoid lumps. Continue cooking for 10 minutes. Season with salt, pepper and nutmeg. Allow to cool.

FILLING

Cook the spinach in a hot frying pan with a little oil until wilted. Drain thoroughly in a colander and roughly chop. Season with salt and pepper. Set aside to cool.

Combine the mozzarella, parmesan and spinach. Add the cold béchamel sauce and adjust the seasoning.

ASSEMBLY

Preheat the oven to 190°C (375°F/Gas 5). Sprinkle a little flour on the work surface. Roll out the dough to a thickness of 3 mm (⅛ inch), and cut out circles with a 14 cm (5½ inch) cutter. Using a 60 ml (2 fl oz/¼ cup) ice-cream scoop or measuring cup, form small balls of filling and place one on each round of dough. Lightly moisten the edge of the dough with a little water and fold over into a half-moon shape. Seal the edges and decorate them with an edging of your choice (see page 26). Set aside in the refrigerator if not cooking immediately.

COOKING

Arrange the empanadas on a baking tray lined with baking paper. Brush with egg yolk and bake for 20 minutes, or until golden and cooked. Allow to cool for a few minutes before serving.

REPULGUE

This spinach filling is one of the most traditional. At Clasico Argentino, it is hidden under the 'verdura' edging, very similar to the 'humita' (see page 26).

CORN & CORIANDER

PREPARATION TIME:
40 MINUTES

RESTING TIME:
2.5 HOURS

COOKING TIME:
55 MINUTES

MAKES 20 EMPANADAS

DOUGH
1 quantity of classic
  dough (see page 20)

BÉCHAMEL
50 g (1¾ oz) unsalted butter
50 g (1¾ oz/⅓ cup) plain
  (all-purpose) flour
500 ml (17 fl oz/2 cups) milk
salt, black pepper
1 pinch of freshly
  grated nutmeg

FILLING
olive oil
1 small onion, sliced
1 red capsicum
  (pepper), diced
500 g (18 oz/2½ cups)
  sweet corn kernels,
  about 6 corn cobs
salt, black pepper
3 teaspoons paprika
1 teaspoon ground
  cinnamon

75 g (2¾ oz/1 small bunch)
  coriander (cilantro)
  leaves, chopped
6 spring onions
  (scallions), chopped

GLAZE
3 egg yolks, beaten

BÉCHAMEL

Melt the butter in a saucepan over low heat. Stir in the flour and mix with a wooden spoon. Cook, stirring, for 4 minutes, then add the milk, stirring constantly to avoid lumps. Continue cooking for 10 minutes. Season with salt, pepper and nutmeg. Allow to cool.

FILLING

Pour a little oil into a hot frying pan and sauté the onion and capsicum for 10 minutes over low heat. Add the corn kernels and continue cooking for 10 minutes. Remove from heat and transfer the mixture to a food processor. Pulse a few times to break up but retain some texture. Refrigerate for 30 minutes.

Combine the corn mixture with the cold béchamel sauce and season with salt, black pepper, paprika and cinnamon. Stir in the coriander and spring onion. Allow filling to rest in the refrigerator for 2 hours.

ASSEMBLY

Preheat the oven to 190°C (375°F/Gas 5). Sprinkle a little flour on the work surface. Roll out the dough to a thickness of 3 mm (⅛ inch), and cut out circles with a 14 cm (5½ inch) cutter. Using a 60 ml (2 fl oz/¼ cup) ice-cream scoop or measuring cup, form small balls of filling and place one on each round of dough. Lightly moisten the edge of the dough with a little water and fold over into a half-moon shape. Seal the edges and give them the 'humita' decoration (see page 26) or an edging of your choice. Set aside in the refrigerator if not cooking immediately.

COOKING

Arrange the empanadas on a baking tray lined with baking paper. Brush with egg yolk and bake for 20 minutes, or until golden and cooked. Allow them to cool for a few minutes before serving.

LEEK

PREPARATION TIME:
30 MINUTES

COOKING TIME:
1 HOUR

MAKES 20 EMPANADAS

DOUGH
1 quantity of puffed
   dough (see page 20)

FILLING
2 large leeks about
   400 g (14 oz) in total,
   white part only
2 French shallots
1 garlic clove

olive oil
1 fresh bay leaf
500 ml (17 fl oz/2 cups)
   chicken stock
250 g (9 oz) raclette cheese
250 g (9 oz) gruyère cheese
250 g (9 oz) mozzarella
   cheese
salt, black pepper

FOR FRYING
1.5 litres (52 fl oz/6 cups)
   sunflower oil

FILLING

Cut the leeks into thin matchsticks. Thinly slice the shallots and crush the garlic.
Pour a little oil into a heavy-based saucepan and sauté the shallot and leek over
low heat for about 5 minutes. Add the garlic, bay leaf and stock and continue cooking
for 30 minutes over low heat, or until most of the liquid has evaporated. Drain off the
remaining liquid. Remove to a container and allow to cool.

Cut the raclette, gruyère and mozzarella into small cubes and combine in a bowl.
Season with salt and pepper and form into small balls of 2 tablespoons each,
compacting them together to the size of a walnut.

ASSEMBLY

Sprinkle a little flour on the work surface. Roll out the dough to a thickness of 3 mm
(⅛ inch). Cut out circles with a 14 cm (5½ inch) cutter. Place 1 tablespoon of the leek
mixture on each round, then a ball of cheese. Lightly moisten the edge of the dough
with a little water and fold over into a half-moon shape. Seal the edges and give them
the 'puerro' decoration (see page 26) or an edging of your choice. Set aside in the
refrigerator if not cooking immediately.

COOKING

In a saucepan or deep-fryer, heat the oil for frying to 180°C (350°F), or until a cube of
bread dropped into the oil turns golden brown in 15 seconds. Add a few empanadas to
the oil, and fry for 5 minutes, or until they brown. Remove from the oil and drain on paper
towels. Repeat this process with the remaining empanadas. Allow them to cool for a few
minutes before serving.

SILVERBEET & PUMPKIN

PREPARATION TIME:
40 MINUTES

COOKING TIME:
55 MINUTES

MAKES 20 EMPANADAS

DOUGH
1 quantity of classic
  dough (see page 20)

BÉCHAMEL
50 g (1¾ oz) unsalted butter
50 g (1¾ oz/⅓ cup) plain
  (all-purpose) flour
500 ml (17 fl oz/2 cups) milk
salt, black pepper

1 pinch of freshly grated
  nutmeg

FILLING
500 g (1 lb 2 oz) silverbeet
  leaves, stalks removed
500 g (1 lb 2 oz) pumpkin
  (winter squash),
  peeled and seeded
1 large onion, thinly sliced

olive oil
a little chicken stock
  (optional)
salt, black pepper
200 g (7 oz) parmesan
  cheese

GLAZE
3 egg yolks

BÉCHAMEL

Melt the butter in a saucepan over low heat. Stir in the flour and mix with a wooden spoon. Cook, stirring, for 4 minutes, then add the milk, stirring constantly to avoid lumps. Continue cooking for 10 minutes. Season with salt, pepper and nutmeg. Allow to cool.

FILLING

Wash the silverbeet and shred finely. Bring a saucepan of salted water to the boil and cook the silverbeet for 5 minutes. Drain and set aside.

Cut the pumpkin flesh into small cubes. Sauté the onion in a frying pan with a little oil over low heat for 5 minutes. Add the pumpkin and cook for a further 8–10 minutes until softened. Add a little stock or water, if needed, to prevent the mixture browning. Season with salt and pepper. Cool.

In a bowl, mix together the silverbeet, pumpkin, cold béchamel sauce and parmesan. Season with salt and pepper.

ASSEMBLY

Preheat the oven to 190°C (375°F/Gas 5). Sprinkle a little flour on the work surface. Roll out the dough to a thickness of 3 mm (⅛ inch), and cut out circles with a 14 cm (5½ inch) cutter. Using a 60 ml (2 fl oz/¼ cup) ice-cream scoop or measuring cup, form small balls of filling and place one on each round of dough. Lightly moisten the edge of the dough with a little water, then fold over into a half-moon shape. Seal the edges and decorate them with an edging of your choice (see page 26). Set aside in the refrigerator if not cooking immediately.

COOKING

Arrange the empanadas on a baking tray lined with baking paper. Brush them with egg yolk and bake for 20 minutes, or until golden and cooked. Allow them to cool for a few minutes before serving.

HAM & CHEESE

PREPARATION TIME:
30 MINUTES

COOKING TIME:
20 MINUTES

MAKES 20 EMPANADAS

DOUGH
1 quantity of classic
   dough (see page 20)

FILLING
450 g (1 lb) raclette
   cheese, rind removed
200 g (7 oz) mozzarella
   cheese

200 g (7 oz) emmental
   cheese
salt, black pepper
10 thin slices of ham (fat
   and rind removed)

GLAZE
3 egg yolks, beaten

FILLING

Cut the raclette and mozzarella into small dice and grate the emmental. Combine the cheeses and season with salt and pepper. Form small balls around 40 g (1½ oz) each, about the size of a walnut. Set aside.

ASSEMBLY

Preheat the oven to 190°C (375°F/Gas 5). Sprinkle a little flour on the work surface. Roll out the dough to a thickness of 3 mm (⅛ inch), and cut out circles with a 14 cm (5½ inch) cutter. Place half a slice of ham, trimming or folding to fit, on each round of dough and top with a portion of cheese. Lightly moisten the edge of the dough with a little water and fold over into a half-moon shape. Seal the edges and give them the 'jamon y queso' decoration (see page 26) or an edging of your choice. Set aside in the refrigerator if not cooking immediately.

COOKING

Arrange the empanadas on a baking tray lined with baking paper. Brush with egg yolk and bake for 20 minutes, or until golden and cooked. Allow them to cool for a few minutes before serving.

SECRET TIP

Wrapping the ham around the cheese helps to hold in the melted cheese so it doesn't run too much.

PORTEÑITA
MOZZARELLA, BACON, PRUNES

PREPARATION TIME:
30 MINUTES

COOKING TIME:
45 MINUTES

MAKES 20 EMPANADAS

DOUGH
1 quantity of puffed
   dough (see page 20)

FILLING
600 g (1 lb 5 oz)
   mozzarella cheese
150 g (5½ oz) Saint-
   Paulin, rind removed,
   or Havarti cheese

salt, black pepper
20 small slices smoked
   streaky bacon (or
   10 long slices halved)
10 prunes, pitted

FOR FRYING
1.5 litres (52 fl oz/6 cups)
   sunflower oil

FILLING

Preheat the oven to 190°C (375°F/Gas 5). Cut the mozzarella and Saint-Paulin into small cubes. Season with salt and pepper.

Lay the slices of bacon on a baking tray lined with baking paper. Bake for 15 minutes, or until golden and cooked.

Cut the prunes in half lengthways. Wrap each half in a slice of bacon. Form balls of cheese using a 60 ml (2 fl oz/¼ cup) ice-cream scoop or measuring cup (loosely packed). Insert a bacon-wrapped prune into each cheese ball and squeeze tightly to bind.

ASSEMBLY

Sprinkle a little flour on the work surface. Roll out the dough to a thickness of 3 mm (⅛ inch), and cut out circles with a 14 cm (5½ inch) cutter. Place a ball of cheese on each round of dough. Lightly moisten the edge of the dough with a little water and fold over into a half-moon shape. Seal the edges and give them the 'jamon y queso' decoration (see page 26) or an edging of your choice. Set aside in the refrigerator if not cooking immediately.

COOKING

In a saucepan or deep-fryer, heat the oil for frying to 180°C (350°F), or until a cube of bread dropped into the oil turns golden brown in 15 seconds. Add a few empanadas to the oil, and fry for 5 minutes, or until they brown. Remove from the oil and drain on paper towels. Repeat this process with the remaining empanadas. Allow them to cool for a few minutes before serving.

FUGAZZETA
CHEESE & ONION

PREPARATION TIME:
35 MINUTES

COOKING TIME:
35 MINUTES

MAKES 20 EMPANADAS

DOUGH
1 quantity of classic
  dough (see page 20)

FILLING
1 tablespoon olive oil
1 large onion, sliced
salt, black pepper
3 tablespoons dried
  oregano

2 tablespoons aji molido
  (see glossary)
250 g (9 oz) gruyère cheese
200 g (7 oz) Saint-
  Paulin, rind removed,
  or Havarti cheese
200 g (7 oz) raclette
  cheese, rind removed

GLAZE
3 egg yolks, beaten

FILLING

Heat the oil in a frying pan. Sauté the onion for 5 minutes over high heat. Lower heat and continue cooking for 10 minutes, or until golden and soft. Set aside in a bowl and allow to cool. Season with salt, pepper, oregano and aji molido.

Grate the gruyère and cut the Saint-Paulin and raclette into 1 cm (½ inch) cubes. Combine the cheeses in a bowl. Form into small balls of about 40 g (1½ oz) or 2 tablespoons.

ASSEMBLY

Preheat the oven to 190°C (375°F/Gas 5). Sprinkle a little flour on the work surface. Roll out the dough to a thickness of 3 mm (⅛ inch), and cut out circles with a 14 cm (5½ inch) cutter. Place a ball of cheese on each round of dough and add 1 teaspoon of cooked onion. Lightly moisten the edge of the dough with a little water and fold over into a half-moon shape. Seal the edges and decorate them with an edging of your choice (see page 26). Set aside in the refrigerator if not cooking immediately.

COOKING

Arrange the empanadas on a baking tray lined with baking paper. Brush with egg yolk and bake for 20 minutes, or until golden and cooked. Allow them to cool for a few minutes before serving.

REPULGUE

At Clasico Argentino, we use a 'queso y cebolla' edging for this filling. It looks like the 'humita' edging on page 26, but the small points are more rounded.

BLUE CHEESE & CELERY

PREPARATION TIME:
30 MINUTES

COOKING TIME:
25 MINUTES

MAKES 20 EMPANADAS

DOUGH
1 quantity of classic
   dough (see page 20)

FILLING
olive oil
125 g (4½ oz/1 cup)
   celery, thinly sliced
   on the diagonal

salt, black pepper
500 g (1 lb 2 oz/4 cups)
   mozzarella cheese, grated
325 g (11½ oz) blue
   cheese, diced
10 pecans, roughly
   chopped

GLAZE
3 egg yolks, beaten

FILLING

Pour a little oil into a hot frying pan and sauté the celery over low heat for 4 minutes, or until soft. Season with salt and pepper. Cool slightly.

In a bowl, combine the mozzarella and blue cheese. Add the celery and work together with a fork to make a smooth mixture. Add the pecans and form small balls using a 60 ml (2 fl oz/¼ cup) ice-cream scoop or measuring cup.

ASSEMBLY

Preheat the oven to 190°C (375°F/Gas 5). Sprinkle a little flour on the work surface. Roll out the dough to a thickness of 3 mm (⅛ inch), and cut out circles with a 14 cm (5½ inch) cutter. Place a ball of cheese mixture on each round of dough. Lightly moisten the edge of the dough with a little water and fold over into a half-moon shape. Seal the edges and decorate them with an edging of your choice (see page 26). Set aside in the refrigerator if not cooking immediately.

COOKING

Arrange the empanadas on a baking tray lined with baking paper. Brush with egg yolk and bake for 20 minutes, or until golden and cooked. Allow them to cool for a few minutes before serving.

CHEESE & MUSHROOM

PREPARATION TIME:
20 MINUTES

COOKING TIME:
30 MINUTES

MAKES 20 EMPANADAS

DOUGH
1 quantity of classic
    dough (see page 20)

FILLING
200 g (7 oz) Saint-
    Paulin, rind removed,
    or Havarti cheese
300 g (10½ oz)
    mozzarella cheese

250 g (9 oz) Comté or
    gruyère cheese
salt, black pepper
150 g (5½ oz) oyster
    mushrooms
150 g (5½ oz) chanterelle
    or other mushrooms
    of choice
150 g (5½ oz) flat or
    button mushrooms

2 French shallots, sliced
olive oil
1 garlic clove, sliced
200 ml (7 fl oz) dry
    white wine

GLAZE
3 egg yolks, beaten

FILLING

Cut the Saint-Paulin and mozzarella into small cubes and grate the Comté. Combine the cheeses and season with salt and pepper.

Wipe and dice the mushrooms. Sauté the shallot in a large frying pan with a little oil over medium heat for 4 minutes without browning. Increase the heat to high. Add the garlic, then the mushroom, and sauté for 5 minutes. Pour in the wine and boil, stirring, for 30 seconds to deglaze the pan, then lower heat and allow the liquid to reduce. Season with salt and pepper. Cool, then combine with the cheese mixture.

ASSEMBLY

Preheat the oven to 190°C (375°F/Gas 5). Sprinkle a little flour on the work surface. Roll out the dough to a thickness of 3 mm (⅛ inch), and cut out circles with a 14 cm (5½ inch) cutter. Using a 60 ml (2 fl oz/¼ cup) ice-cream scoop or measuring cup, form the cheese and mushroom filling into balls and place one on each round of dough. Lightly moisten the edge of the dough with a little water and fold over into a half-moon shape. Seal the edges and decorate them with an edging of your choice (see page 26). Set aside in the refrigerator if not cooking immediately.

COOKING

Arrange the empanadas on a baking tray lined with baking paper. Brush with egg yolk and bake for 20 minutes, or until golden and cooked. Allow them to cool for a few minutes before serving.

CAPRESE
TOMATO, MOZZARELLA, BASIL

PREPARATION TIME:
30 MINUTES

COOKING TIME:
20 MINUTES

MAKES 20 EMPANADAS

DOUGH
1 quantity of classic
 dough (see page 20)

FILLING
300 g (10½ oz) mozzarella
 cheese
225 g (8 oz) scamorza
 cheese (smoked
 mozzarella)

225 g (8 oz) Saint-Paulin,
 rind removed, or Havarti
 cheese
salt, black pepper
200 g (7 oz) semi-dried
 (sun-blushed) tomatoes,
 finely diced
1 handful basil leaves,
 chopped

1 tablespoon cornflour
 (cornstarch)

GLAZE
3 egg yolks, beaten

FILLING

Cut the mozzarella, scamorza and Saint-Paulin into small cubes. Season with salt and pepper and combine with the semi-dried tomato, basil and cornflour. Work the mixture together with your hands.

ASSEMBLY

Preheat the oven to 190°C (375°F/Gas 5). Sprinkle a little flour on the work surface. Roll out the dough to a thickness of 3 mm (⅛ inch), and cut out circles with a 14 cm (5½ inch) cutter. Using a 60 ml (2 fl oz/¼ cup) ice-cream scoop or measuring cup, form the cheese filling into balls and place one on each round of dough. Lightly moisten the edge of the dough with a little water and fold over into a half-moon shape. Seal the edges and decorate them with an edging of your choice (see page 26). Set aside in the refrigerator if not cooking immediately.

COOKING

Arrange the empanadas on a baking tray lined with baking paper. Brush with egg yolk and bake for 20 minutes, or until golden and cooked. Allow them to cool for a few minutes before serving.

LEMON TUNA

PREPARATION TIME:
30 MINUTES

RESTING TIME:
2 HOURS

COOKING TIME:
50 MINUTES

MAKES 20 EMPANADAS

DOUGH
1 quantity of classic
dough (see page 20)

FILLING
3 tablespoons capers,
rinsed and chopped
finely grated zest and
juice of 3 lemons

1 handful flat-leaf (Italian)
parsley, chopped
1 large onion, cut into
matchsticks
1 green capsicum (pepper),
cut into matchsticks
olive oil
1 fresh small green
chilli, finely diced

3 tablespoons tomato paste
(concentrated purée)
200 ml (7 fl oz) fish
stock or water
500 g (1 lb 2 oz) tinned
tuna, drained weight
salt, black pepper

GLAZE
3 egg yolks, beaten

FILLING

Combine the capers, lemon zest and juice and the parsley in a bowl and set aside in the refrigerator.

Sauté the onion and capsicum in a saucepan with a little oil over medium heat without browning. Add the chilli and cook for 10 minutes over low heat. Add the tomato paste and stir well. Add the stock and cook over low heat for 15–20 minutes, or until the liquid has completely evaporated.

Transfer the mixture to a large bowl and combine with the tuna and the caper, lemon and parsley mixture. Season with salt and pepper. Set aside in the refrigerator for 2 hours.

ASSEMBLY

Preheat the oven to 190°C (375°F/Gas 5). Sprinkle a little flour on the work surface. Roll out the dough to a thickness of 3 mm (⅛ inch), and cut out circles with a 14 cm (5½ inch) cutter. Using a 60 ml (2 fl oz/¼ cup) ice-cream scoop or measuring cup, form a portion of filling and place one on each round of dough. Lightly moisten the edge of the dough with a little water and fold over into a half-moon shape. Seal the edges and decorate them with an edging of your choice (see page 26). Set aside in the refrigerator if not cooking immediately.

COOKING

Arrange the empanadas on a baking tray lined with baking paper. Brush with egg yolk and bake for 20 minutes, or until golden and cooked. Allow them to cool for a few minutes before serving.

REPULGUE

At Clasico Argentino, we use an 'atun' edging for this tuna filling. It is quite simple and very smooth, the edges of the empanada are just sealed together.

PRAWN & AVOCADO

PREPARATION TIME:
30 MINUTES

COOKING TIME:
25 MINUTES

MAKES 20 EMPANADAS

DOUGH
1 quantity of puffed
  dough (see page 20)

FILLING
700 g (1 lb 9 oz) raw prawns
  (shrimp), peeled and
  deveined, tails removed
1 red onion, thinly sliced
1 garlic clove, thinly sliced

1 pinch of paprika
1 handful coriander
  (cilantro) leaves, chopped
1 avocado, diced
3 tablespoons
  mascarpone cheese
200 g (7 oz) Manchego
  cheese, grated
finely grated zest of 2 limes
salt, black pepper

FOR FRYING
1.5 litres (52 fl oz/6 cups)
  sunflower oil

FILLING

Bring a saucepan of salted water to the boil and blanch the prawns for 1 minute. Drain and cool in iced water, then cut the prawns into small pieces.

In a bowl, combine the prawn, onion, garlic, paprika and coriander. Add the avocado and mascarpone. Stir in the Manchego cheese and the lime zest. Season with salt and pepper.

ASSEMBLY

Sprinkle a little flour on the work surface. Roll out the dough to a thickness of 3 mm (⅛ inch), and cut out circles with a 14 cm (5½ inch) cutter. Using a 60 ml (2 fl oz/¼ cup) ice-cream scoop or measuring cup, form a portion of filling and place one on each round of dough. Lightly moisten the edge of the dough with a little water and fold over into a half-moon shape. Seal the edges and decorate them with an edging of your choice (see page 26). Set aside in the refrigerator if not cooking immediately.

COOKING

In a saucepan or deep-fryer, heat the oil for frying to 180°C (350°F), or until a cube of bread dropped into the oil turns golden brown in 15 seconds. Add a few empanadas to the oil, and fry for 5 minutes, or until they brown. Remove from the oil and drain on paper towels. Repeat this process with the remaining empanadas. Allow them to cool for a few minutes before serving.

CALAMAR

PREPARATION TIME:
40 MINUTES

RESTING TIME (OPTIONAL):
4 HOURS

COOKING TIME:
50 MINUTES

MAKES 20 EMPANADAS

DOUGH
1 quantity of classic
dough (see page 20)

FILLING
1 kg (2 lb 4 oz) squid
1 onion
1 green capsicum (pepper)
1 fresh small red chilli
3 garlic cloves

olive oil
3 tablespoons tomato paste
(concentrated purée)
200 ml (7 fl oz) dry white
wine
200 ml (7 fl oz) fish stock
or water, if needed
1 handful coriander
(cilantro) leaves, chopped

1 handful flat-leaf (Italian)
parsley, chopped
salt, black pepper

GLAZE
3 egg yolks, beaten

TO SERVE
green chimichurri sauce
(see page 28)

FILLING

Clean and dry the squid and cut into small pieces.

Cut the onion, capsicum, chilli and garlic into a small dice and sauté in a hot frying
pan with a little oil over medium heat. Add the tomato paste and stir to combine.
Pour in the wine and stir for 30 seconds to deglaze the pan, then lower heat and reduce
for 3 minutes.

Stir in the squid and cook over low heat for 20 minutes. Add a little stock if necessary
to prevent the vegetables from browning. Remove from heat. Add the coriander and
parsley and season with salt and pepper. Refrigerate for 4 hours, if possible.

ASSEMBLY

Preheat the oven to 190°C (375°F/Gas 5). Sprinkle a little flour on the work surface.
Roll out the dough to a thickness of 3 mm (⅛ inch), and cut out circles with a 14 cm
(5½ inch) cutter. Using a 60 ml (2 fl oz/¼ cup) ice-cream scoop or measuring cup, form
a portion of filling and place one on each round of dough. Lightly moisten the edge of
the dough with a little water and fold over into a half-moon shape. Seal the edges and
decorate them with an edging of your choice (see page 26). Set aside in the refrigerator
if not cooking immediately.

COOKING

Arrange the empanadas on a baking tray lined with baking paper. Brush with egg
yolk and bake for 20 minutes, or until golden and cooked. Allow them to cool for a few
minutes before serving. Serve with the green chimichurri sauce.

MINI EMPANADAS
DULCE DE LECHE

PREPARATION TIME:
20 MINUTES

COOKING TIME:
12–15 MINUTES

MAKES 30 EMPANADAS

DOUGH
1 quantity of classic
  dough (see page 20)

FILLING
450 g (1 lb) dulce de
  leche (see page 136,
  or ready-made)

GLAZE
3 egg yolks, beaten

TO SERVE
300 ml (10½ fl oz) thin
  (pouring) cream
100 g (3½ oz) icing
  (confectioners') sugar

ASSEMBLY

Preheat the oven to 190°C (375°F/Gas 5). Sprinkle a little flour on the work surface.
Roll out the dough to a thickness of 3 mm (⅛ inch), and cut out circles with an 8 cm
(3¼ inch) cutter. Top each round of dough with 2 teaspoons (15 g/½ oz) of dulce de
leche. Lightly moisten the edge of the dough with a little water and fold over into a
half-moon shape. Seal the edges and decorate them with an edging of your choice
(see page 26). Set aside in the refrigerator if not cooking immediately.

COOKING

Arrange the empanadas on a baking tray lined with baking paper. Brush with egg
yolk and bake for 12–15 minutes, or until golden and cooked. Allow them to cool for
a few minutes before serving. Whip the cream and icing sugar until thick to serve with
the empanadas.

PASTELITO DE BATATA
SWEET POTATO PASTE

PREPARATION TIME:
20 MINUTES

COOKING TIME:
12–15 MINUTES

MAKES 12 PASTELITOS

DOUGH
500 g (1 lb 2 oz/3⅓ cups)
plain (all-purpose) flour
10 g (¼ oz) fine sea salt
160 g (5¾ oz) unsalted
butter
170 ml (5½ fl oz/⅔ cup)
water, approx

FILLING
12 slices of dulce de batata,
6 x 3 cm (2½ x 1¼ inches)
(see note below)

GLAZE
3 egg yolks, beaten

TO SERVE
icing (confectioners') sugar
chocolate sauce
(see page 104)

DOUGH

Make the classic dough for baking by following the instructions on page 20, but using the quantities given above.

ASSEMBLY

Preheat the oven to 180°C (350°F/Gas 4). Sprinkle a little flour on the work surface. Roll out the dough to a thickness of 3 mm (⅛ inch), and cut out circles with a 9 cm (3½ inch) cutter. Top each round of dough with a slice of dulce de batata. Fold the edges inward and roll forward to close. Set aside in the refrigerator if not cooking immediately.

COOKING

Arrange the pastelitos on a baking tray lined with baking paper. Brush with egg yolk and bake for 12–15 minutes, or until golden and cooked. Allow them to cool for 15 minutes before serving. Dust with icing sugar and serve with chocolate sauce.

DULCE DE BATATA

Dulce de batata is a sweet potato paste. It's a sweet jelly, like a dense jam, and traditionally dark in colour, like caramel. You can find it in Argentinian and speciality food stores.

PASTELITO DE MEMBRILLO

PREPARATION TIME:
30 MINUTES

COOKING TIME:
15 MINUTES

MAKES 20 PASTELITOS

DOUGH
40 x 8 cm (3¼ inch) squares
    of puff pastry (about
    1 kg/2 lb 4 oz puff pastry)

FILLING
20 x 3 cm (1¼ inch)
    squares of quince paste

GLAZE
3 egg yolks

TO SERVE
icing (confectioners') sugar
ice cream (optional)

ASSEMBLY

Preheat the oven to 180°C (350°F/Gas 4). Place a square of quince paste on a square of puff pastry. Cover with a second square of puff pastry so the corners form an 8-pointed star (see the pastelito edging on page 26). Pinch each end together while keeping the star shape of the pastelito. Repeat this process with the other squares of pastry and quince paste.

COOKING

Arrange the pastelitos on a baking tray lined with baking paper and brush with egg yolk. Bake for 15 minutes, or until puffed and golden. Dust with icing sugar when they come out of the oven and allow to cool. Serve with a scoop of ice cream or simply as a sweet snack.

APPLE, PEAR & PINEAPPLE

PREPARATION TIME:
30 MINUTES

RESTING TIME:
1 HOUR

COOKING TIME:
15–20 MINUTES

MAKES 20 EMPANADAS

DOUGH
220 g (7¾ oz) unsalted
  butter, softened
270 g (9½ oz) caster
  (superfine) sugar
2 eggs
500 g (1 lb 2 oz/3⅓ cups)
  plain (all-purpose) flour
5 g (⅛ oz) fine sea salt

FILLING
½ pineapple, about
  500 g (1 lb 2 oz)
1 golden delicious apple
1 pear
1 tablespoon unsalted
  butter
100 g (3½ oz/½ cup lightly
  packed) soft brown sugar

finely grated zest of 1 orange
finely grated zest of 1 lemon
30 g (1 oz/¼ cup)
  chopped nuts
4 tablespoons apricot jam

GLAZE
3 egg yolks, beaten

DOUGH

Combine the softened butter with the sugar. Add the eggs, one at a time, then the sifted flour and salt. Work the mixture as little as possible and cover the dough with plastic wrap. Let the dough rest for at least 1 hour in the refrigerator.

FILLING

Peel the pineapple, apple and pear and cut into small cubes. Sauté gently in a large saucepan with the butter, over high heat. Sprinkle with brown sugar and allow it to caramelise for 5 minutes. Pour the fruit mixture onto a tray and add the orange and lemon zest and the nuts. Allow to cool, then add the apricot jam and stir through.

ASSEMBLY

Preheat the oven to 180°C (350°F/Gas 4). Sprinkle a little flour on the work surface. Roll out the dough to a thickness of 3 mm (⅛ inch), and cut out circles with an 8 cm (3¼ inch) cutter. Top each round of dough with 1 tablespoon of filling. Lightly moisten the edge of the dough with a little water and fold over into a half-moon shape. Seal the edges and decorate them with an edging of your choice (see page 26). Set aside in the refrigerator if not cooking immediately.

COOKING

Arrange the empanadas on a baking tray lined with baking paper. Brush with egg yolk and bake for 15–20 minutes, or until golden and cooked. Allow them to cool for 15 minutes before serving.

BANANA ROLLS
WITH SPICES & COCONUT

PREPARATION TIME:
20 MINUTES

COOKING TIME:
16–19 MINUTES

MAKES 20 ROLLS

DOUGH
1 quantity of classic
  dough (see page 20)

FILLING
10 small bananas
2 tablespoons soft
  brown sugar
finely grated zest of 2 limes

2 tablespoons desiccated
  (shredded) coconut
2 teaspoons ground star
  anise
1 pinch of ground
  cardamom
seeds from 1 vanilla bean
1 tablespoon almond meal

2 teaspoons ground
  cinnamon
1 pinch of fine sea salt

GLAZE
3 egg yolks, beaten
icing (confectioners') sugar

FILLING

Cut the bananas in half lengthways and trim to a maximum length of 8 cm (3¼ inches). Combine the sugar, lime zest, coconut, star anise, cardamom, vanilla seeds, almond meal, cinnamon and salt in a bowl. Roll the pieces of banana in the spice mixture and set aside.

ASSEMBLY

Preheat the oven to 180°C (350°F/Gas 4). Sprinkle a little flour on the work surface. Roll out the dough to a thickness of 3 mm (⅛ inch), and cut out circles with a 14 cm (5½ inch) cutter. Place each banana half on a round. Fold the edges inward and roll forward to give the shape of a roll (like a spring roll—see the 'choriempa' fold page 26).

COOKING

Arrange the rolls on a baking tray lined with baking paper. Brush with egg yolk and bake for 12–15 minutes. Remove the tray from the oven and sprinkle each roll with icing sugar. Return to the oven for 4 minutes to caramelise. Allow to cool slightly before serving.

SERVING

This dish can be served with vanilla or zabaglione ice cream.

LOS PICA PICA

LITTLE DISHES

CARPACCIOS / PRESERVES

TIRADITO DE LOMO ARGENTINO

PREPARATION TIME:
25 MINUTES

RESTING TIME:
1 HOUR

SERVES 4

THE MEAT
600 g (1 lb 5 oz) very
   fresh beef eye fillet

MARINADE
1 red onion, finely diced
2–3 cm (¾–1¼ inch)
   piece of ginger, grated
1 handful coriander
   (cilantro) leaves, chopped

1 celery stalk, diced
juice of 2 limes
salt, black pepper

TO SERVE
1 avocado, diced
a few celery leaves
a drizzle of vinaigrette
fine sea salt
freshly ground black pepper

THE MEAT

Lay some plastic wrap on the work surface. Place the eye fillet on top and wrap tightly with the plastic wrap to make a sausage shape. Seal the ends tightly and place the meat in the freezer for about 1 hour: it needs to be partly frozen so it can be sliced thinly.

MARINADE

Combine all the ingredients in a bowl. Season with salt and pepper.

SERVING

Unwrap the fillet and slice thinly. Sprinkle four plates with salt and pepper and lay out the slices of beef without overlapping them too much. Pour a quarter of the marinade over the meat on each plate. Let it 'cook' for 5 minutes. Top with a little avocado, some celery leaves and a drizzle of vinaigrette. Season with sea salt and freshly ground black pepper.

DUCK BREAST
'LIKE A HAM'

PREPARATION TIME:
30 MINUTES

RESTING TIME:
24 HOURS

SERVES 6

DUCK
3 duck breast fillets, skin on
3 star anise
2 cinnamon sticks
4 cloves
1 tablespoon black
   peppercorns
1 tablespoon coriander
   seeds
2 kg (4 lb 8 oz) coarse
   rock salt

1 kg (2 lb 4 oz) sugar

ONIONS
2 red onions
200 ml (7 fl oz) white
   wine vinegar
3 tablespoons soft
   brown sugar

TO SERVE
1 pear, cut into strips
a handful of herbs
   (selection of parsley,
   tarragon, coriander, basil)
olive oil
freshly ground black pepper

DUCK BREAST

Trim the duck and remove any excess fat and sinew. Set aside.

Crush the spices using a mortar and pestle. Mix the salt, sugar and spice mixture together in a bowl.

Spread a third of this mixture in a shallow dish or tray, a little larger than the three duck breasts and lay the duck on top. Fully cover the duck with the remaining spice mixture and cover with plastic wrap. Refrigerate for 24 hours.

ONIONS

Peel and thinly slice the onions. Pour the vinegar and brown sugar into a bowl. Stir to dissolve the sugar completely. Add the onion, toss to coat, and refrigerate for 24 hours.

SERVING

The next day, rinse the duck in cold water and dry with paper towels. Cut into thin slices and divide between six plates. Serve with strips of pear and garnish with the onion. Top with herbs, a drizzle of oil and freshly ground black pepper.

BURRATA DI BUFALA
& GRATED TOMATOES

PREPARATION TIME:
20 MINUTES

RESTING TIME:
20 MINUTES

SERVES 4

TOMATOES
4 tomatoes
1 garlic clove
80 ml (2½ fl oz/
⅓ cup) olive oil
fine sea salt
black pepper

BURRATA
4 *burrata di bufala*,
(Buffalo Mozarella)
fine sea salt
black pepper
olive oil
8–12 anchovies
12 semi-dried (sun-
blushed) tomatoes

TOMATOES

Grate the tomato and garlic into a bowl. Add the oil, salt and pepper. Set aside in the refrigerator for 20 minutes.

SERVING

Place a *burrata* on each of four plates or bowls. Dress with a little of the tomato mixture. Season with sea salt and pepper and a little oil. Place 2–3 anchovies and 3 semi-dried tomatoes on each plate or bowl.

MARINATED ARTICHOKES

PREPARATION TIME:
30 MINUTES

COOKING TIME:
15 MINUTES

SERVES 4

INGREDIENTS

juice of 2 lemons +
  1 lemon extra
12 small artichokes
1 tablespoon black
  peppercorns
200 ml (7 fl oz)
  sherry vinegar

500 ml (17 fl oz/2 cups)
  olive oil
a few leaves of flat-leaf
  (Italian) parsley
salt, black pepper

ARTICHOKES

Add the lemon juice to a bowl of water. Trim the stem of the artichoke, leaving about 3 cm (1¼ inches). Remove the outside leaves so only the heart and stem remains. Plunge them into the lemon water so they don't oxidise.

COOKING

Bring a large saucepan of water to the boil and cook the artichokes for 10 minutes. They should be cooked but still firm. Plunge immediately into a bowl of iced water.

MARINATING

Cut the extra lemon into slices. Place a few slices of lemon, some peppercorns, vinegar, oil and a few leaves of parsley in a jar and alternate with the artichokes until the whole jar is filled. Season with salt and black pepper.

STORING

You can enjoy the artichokes immediately. They will keep for 10 days in the refrigerator.

BEETROOT
& FRESH GOAT'S CHEESE

PREPARATION TIME:
20 MINUTES

COOKING TIME:
30 MINUTES

SERVES 6

BEETROOT
2 red beetroot (beets)
2 yellow beetroot (beets)
1 Chioggia (striped)
  beetroot (beet), or replace
  with 1 of the above

MARINADE
1 tablespoon coriander
  seeds
1 tablespoon black
  peppercorns
a few sprigs of dill
200 ml (7 fl oz) white
  wine vinegar
olive oil

TO SERVE
300 g (10½ oz) fresh goat's
  cheese (curd style)
3 tablespoons coarsely
  chopped pistachios
salt, black pepper

BEETROOT

Bring a saucepan of salted water to the boil and cook the unpeeled red and yellow beetroot for about 30 minutes, until cooked but still firm. Cool, then peel and cut into thin slices. Set aside. Peel the raw Chioggia, if using, and slice very thinly with a mandolin. Set aside.

MARINADE

Place the coriander seeds, peppercorns and dill in a jar or container large enough to hold all the beetroot. Add the vinegar and the beetroot, and fill the jar with oil to the rim, or cover the beetroot with oil in the container. Seal the jar or place the lid on the container.

SERVING

Combine the goat's cheese with the pistachios (reserving a few for garnish). Season with salt and pepper. Serve the beetroot in shallow bowls. Dress with the cheese mixture and scatter over the reserved pistachios just before serving.

STORING
The marinated beetroot will keep in the refrigerator for at least 5 days.

LOS HELADOS

ICE CREAMS

ICE CREAMS / SORBETS / SUNDAES

ICE CREAM

THE TRADITION OF ICE CREAM IN ARGENTINA

How can we talk about Argentina and its food without mentioning the *helados*? Ice cream is as widespread in Buenos Aires as the empanada. And connoisseurs would have to agree that Argentinian ice cream is among the best in the world!

In Argentina, enormous amounts of ice cream are consumed every day. Day and night, summer and winter, ice cream is part of the daily diet: *helado* is one of the symbols of Argentinian cuisine. *Heladerias* have overtaken the cities—it's impossible to go for a walk without coming across an ice-cream shop!

THE FLAVOURS

There are hundreds of flavours of ice cream in Argentina, half of which are based on dulce de leche. Our flavours include raspberry–Malbec, zabaglione, chocolate and, of course, dulce de leche. Discover the secrets of this legendary and deliciously flavoured ice cream.

THE SECRETS OF ARGENTINIAN ICE CREAM

INSPIRED BY THE ITALIAN RECIPE, ARGENTINIAN ICE CREAM HAS A SPECIAL SMOOTHNESS. GOOD INGREDIENTS ARE CRUCIAL FOR SUCCESS. AS ALL ICE-CREAM MAKERS WILL TELL YOU, IT TAKES MORE THAN A GOOD ICE-CREAM MACHINE TO MAKE GOOD ICE CREAM!

THE INGREDIENTS

At Clasico Argentino, the ice creams are made from full-cream milk, dulce de leche imported from Argentina, vanilla beans and fruit that's carefully chosen for optimum sweetness. There are also a few rather specialised ingredients that are essential for the creaminess of genuine Argentinian ice cream and that ensure a longer shelf life.

INVERT SUGAR SYRUP: a form of sugar that has powerful sweetening properties and delays the freezing process and the formation of ice crystals. (Using normal caster (superfine) sugar might result in a crystallised ice cream.)

DEXTROSE: a low-sweetness sugar that helps prevent the formation of ice crystals. It allows you to make an ice cream that's not as sweet but still creamy.

FRUIT PURÉE: 100% fruit preparation found in speciality pastry-making stores. You can make purées at home in a blender with fresh fruit.

STABILISERS: elements that improve the emulsion of the ice cream and prevent the formation of ice crystals, so the ice creams keep for a longer time.

All of these products can be easily found at speciality food stores or on websites of businesses specialising in pastry-making supplies. You can make the recipes using traditional ingredients (the vanilla ice cream works very well without the above, for example), but the quality may not be as good.

THE TECHNIQUES

The way the ingredients are handled is very important for achieving a smooth and creamy texture. When you observe the maturing period in the refrigerator and the full cooling cycle, it produces a result that is incomparable with mass-produced ice creams. Although Clasico Argentino uses a professional ice cream–making machine, the recipes in this book give you the secrets to making successful ice cream at home.

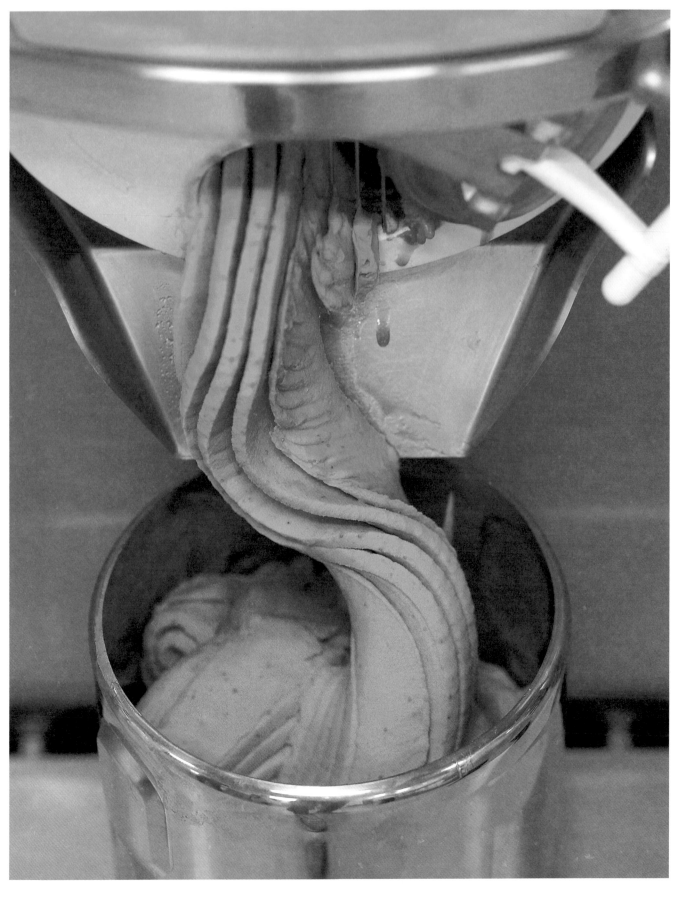

SAUCES & TOPPINGS

Clasico Argentino has developed its own house toppings for embellishing its ice creams: chocolate crumble, its famous garrapiñadas (praline almonds, see page 144), and preserved cumquats (see page 146). Chocolate chips (dark or white chocolate) and fresh cut fruit are also on hand. Finally, discover the best sauces for topping sorbets and ice creams.

CHOCOLATE SAUCE

 PREPARATION TIME:
10 MINUTES

 COOKING TIME:
8 MINUTES

MAKES 1 LITRE
(35 FL OZ/4 CUPS)

INGREDIENTS
300 g (10½ oz) caster (superfine) sugar
600 ml (21 fl oz) water
60 g (2¼ oz) coffee beans
50 g (1¾ oz/⅓ cup) dark chocolate (70% cocoa), chopped

160 g (5¾ oz/1½ cups) unsweetened cocoa powder

Combine the sugar, water and coffee beans in a saucepan. Bring to the boil, stirring to dissolve the sugar. Add the chocolate and cocoa powder and stir constantly. When the sauce is smooth, strain into a bowl through a sieve, cover the surface with plastic wrap and refrigerate until cold. Once chilled, store in an airtight container in the refrigerator for up to 5 days.

DULCE DE LECHE SAUCE

 PREPARATION TIME:
10 MINUTES

MAKES 450 ML (16 FL OZ)

INGREDIENTS
300 g (10½ oz) dulce de leche (see page 136, or ready-made)

200 ml (7 fl oz) milk
1 tablespoon cognac

Put the dulce de leche into a bowl. Gradually incorporate the milk with a whisk until you reach the desired consistency. Add the cognac to finish. Store in the refrigerator.

CHOCOLATE CRUMBLE

 PREPARATION TIME:
15 MINUTES

 COOKING TIME:
15–20 MINUTES

MAKES 2¾ CUPS

INGREDIENTS
125 g (4½ oz) caster (superfine) sugar
125 g (4½ oz/1¼ cups) almond meal
75 g (2¾ oz/½ cup) plain (all-purpose) flour

50 g (1¾ oz) unsweetened cocoa powder
½ teaspoon fine sea salt
70 g (2½ oz) unsalted butter, melted

Preheat the oven to 150°C (300°F/Gas 2). Mix the sugar, almond meal, flour, cocoa powder and salt together and stir in the melted butter with a wooden spoon until you have a moist, sandy texture. Spread the mixture out on a baking tray lined with baking paper and bake for 15–20 minutes. Cool on the tray then store in an airtight container. The crumble keeps for one week. Use as a topping for sundaes and desserts.

DULCE DE LECHE
ICE CREAM

PREPARATION TIME:
15 MINUTES

COOKING TIME:
5 MINUTES

REFRIGERATION TIME:
3–6 HOURS

MAKES 1 LITRE
(35 FL OZ/4 CUPS)

INGREDIENTS

1 tablespoon caster
  (superfine) sugar
1 tablespoon dextrose
5 g (⅛ oz) ice-cream
  stabiliser (optional)
500 ml (17 fl oz/2 cups) milk
350 g (12 oz) dulce de
  leche (see page 136,
  or ready-made)

Combine the sugar, dextrose and stabiliser, if using. Heat the milk in a saucepan to just below boiling and add the dry ingredients in a steady stream, whisking to prevent lumps forming. Put the dulce de leche in a heatproof bowl, pour over the hot milk mixture and mix with a hand blender until well combined. Transfer to a container. Cover the surface with plastic wrap and refrigerate for 3–6 hours.

Churn in an ice-cream maker according to the manufacturer's instructions. Serve immediately or store in the freezer.

VANILLA
ICE CREAM

 PREPARATION TIME:
30 MINUTES

 COOKING TIME:
10 MINUTES

 REFRIGERATION TIME:
3–6 HOURS

MAKES 1 LITRE
(35 FL OZ/4 CUPS)

INGREDIENTS
seeds from 4 vanilla beans
400 ml (14 fl oz) milk
450 ml (16 fl oz) thin
   (pouring) cream
1 tablespoon coffee beans
6 egg yolks
150 g (5½ oz/⅔ cup)
   caster (superfine) sugar

Combine the vanilla seeds, milk, cream and coffee beans in a saucepan and heat over medium heat. Remove from heat just before boiling point.

Whisk the egg yolks and sugar in a bowl until well combined. Pour the infused milk over this mixture, whisking to combine.

Strain the mixture through a sieve and return to the saucepan. Cook over medium heat, stirring constantly, until the custard coats the back of a wooden spoon and you can run your finger through it leaving a clear trace. Transfer to a container. Cover the surface with plastic wrap and refrigerate for 3–6 hours.

Churn in an ice-cream maker according to the manufacturer's instructions. Serve immediately or store in the freezer.

SECRET TIP
Infusing the full-bodied flavour of coffee beans into the
vanilla ice cream gives it more depth.

CHOCOLATE
ICE CREAM

PREPARATION TIME:
10 MINUTES

COOKING TIME:
10 MINUTES

REFRIGERATION TIME:
3–6 HOURS

MAKES 1 LITRE
(35 FL OZ/4 CUPS)

BASE INGREDIENTS
500 ml (17 fl oz/2 cups) milk
125 ml (4 fl oz/½ cup) thin
   (pouring) cream
   (35% dairy fat)
100 g (3½ oz) invert
   sugar syrup
1 egg yolk

DRY INGREDIENTS
30 g (1 oz/¼ cup) skim
   milk powder (0% fat)
70 g (2½ oz) good
   quality unsweetened
   cocoa powder
5 g (⅛ oz) ice-cream
   stabiliser (optional)
100 g (3½ oz) dextrose

Combine the dry ingredients in a bowl. Add the milk and cream, then mix with a hand blender or a whisk. Once the mixture is well blended, add the invert sugar syrup and egg yolk. Pour the mixture into a saucepan and heat gently, stirring until the mixture is smooth and combined.

Pour the mixture into a bowl, cover the surface with plastic wrap and refrigerate for 3–6 hours.

Churn the mixture in an ice-cream maker according to the manufacturer's instructions. Serve immediately or store in the freezer.

ZABAGLIONE
ICE CREAM

PREPARATION TIME:
15 MINUTES

COOKING TIME:
10 MINUTES

REFRIGERATION TIME:
3–6 HOURS

MAKES 1 LITRE
(35 FL OZ/4 CUPS)

BASE INGREDIENTS
400 ml (14 fl oz) milk
200 ml (7 fl oz) thin
  (pouring) cream
  (35% dairy fat)
5 egg yolks
180 ml (6 fl oz/¾ cup)
  sweet Marsala wine

DRY INGREDIENTS
130 g (4½ oz) caster
  (superfine) sugar
50 g (1¾ oz) skim milk
  powder (0% fat)
5 g (⅛ oz) ice-cream
  stabiliser (optional)

Combine the dry ingredients in a bowl.

Combine the milk, cream, egg yolks and Marsala in a saucepan. Place over medium heat. Add the dry ingredients in a steady stream and whisk vigorously to prevent lumps forming. Cook, stirring constantly, for 10 minutes, or until it reaches just below boiling point (about 85°C/185°F on a sugar thermometer). The mixture will be ready when it coats the back of a wooden spoon and you can run your finger through it leaving a clear trace. Strain through a sieve, cover the surface with plastic wrap and refrigerate for 3–6 hours.

Churn the mixture in an ice-cream maker according to the manufacturer's instructions. Serve immediately or store in the freezer.

ZABAGLIONE

Zabaglione is a preparation based on egg yolks and Marsala wine, which traditionally takes the form of a cream or custard. It is also a variety of ice cream.

STRAWBERRY
SORBET

 PREPARATION TIME:
15 MINUTES

 COOKING TIME:
5 MINUTES

 REFRIGERATION TIME:
1–2 HOURS

MAKES 1 LITRE
(35 FL OZ/4 CUPS)

BASE INGREDIENTS
250 ml (9 fl oz/1 cup) water
juice of 1 lemon
500 g (1 lb 2 oz/3⅓ cups)
   hulled strawberries

DRY INGREDIENTS
240 g (8½ oz) caster
   (superfine) sugar
5 g (⅛ oz) sorbet
   stabiliser (optional)

Mix the sugar with the stabiliser, if using. Bring the water to a boil in a saucepan. Remove from heat. Add the dry ingredients in a steady stream, stirring until the sugar has dissolved. Add the lemon juice.

Pour the syrup into a container and allow to cool completely in the refrigerator for 1–2 hours.

Purée the strawberries in a blender or food processor, add the syrup and process to combine.

Churn the mixture in an ice-cream maker according to the manufacturer's instructions. Serve immediately or store in the freezer.

RASPBERRY-MALBEC
SORBET

PREPARATION TIME:
15 MINUTES

COOKING TIME:
5 MINUTES

REFRIGERATION TIME:
1–2 HOURS

MAKES 1 LITRE
(35 FL OZ/4 CUPS)

BASE INGREDIENTS
200 ml (7 fl oz) water
400 g (14 oz) raspberries
200 ml (7 fl oz) Malbec
  wine, chilled

DRY INGREDIENTS
200 g (7 oz) caster
  (superfine) sugar
5 g (⅛ oz) sorbet
  stabiliser (optional)

Mix the sugar with the stabiliser, if using. Bring the water to a boil in a saucepan.
Remove from heat. Add the dry ingredients in a steady stream, stirring until the sugar
has dissolved.

Pour the syrup into a bowl and allow to cool completely in the refrigerator for 1–2 hours,
or until chilled.

Purée the raspberries in a blender or food processor with the syrup and the Malbec.
Push the mixture through a sieve to remove the seeds if desired.

Churn in an ice-cream maker according to the manufacturer's instructions. Serve
immediately or store in the freezer.

MALBEC
Malbec is a variety of red wine that's very common in Argentina, and it goes
particularly well with berries. It can be found in liquor stores.

MANGO SORBET

PREPARATION TIME:
10 MINUTES

COOKING TIME:
5 MINUTES

REFRIGERATION TIME:
1–2 HOURS

MAKES 1 LITRE
(35 FL OZ/4 CUPS)

BASE INGREDIENTS
300 ml (10½ fl oz) water
450 g (1 lb) mango flesh

DRY INGREDIENTS
235 g (8½ oz) caster
  (superfine) sugar
5 g (⅛ oz) sorbet
  stabiliser (optional)

Mix the sugar with the stabiliser, if using. Heat the water in a saucepan over a low heat. Add the dry ingredients in a steady stream, stirring until the sugar has dissolved. Transfer to a container and refrigerate for 1–2 hours.

Purée the mango in a blender or food processor with the syrup.

Churn in an ice-cream maker according to the manufacturer's instructions. Serve immediately or store in the freezer.

BANANA SORBET

PREPARATION TIME:
10 MINUTES

COOKING TIME:
5 MINUTES

REFRIGERATION TIME:
1–2 HOURS

MAKES 1 LITRE
(35 FL OZ/4 CUPS)

BASE INGREDIENTS
400 ml (14 fl oz) water
2½ tablespoons lemon juice
350 g (12 oz) banana
  flesh (about 2 bananas)
  + 1 banana

DRY INGREDIENTS
210 g (7½ oz) caster
  (superfine) sugar

5 g (⅛ oz) sorbet
  stabiliser (optional)

Mix the sugar with the stabiliser, if using. Heat the water in a saucepan over a low heat. Add the dry ingredients in a steady stream, stirring until the sugar has dissolved. Add the lemon juice. Transfer to a container and refrigerate for 1–2 hours.

Purée the 350 g (12 oz) banana in a blender or food processor with the syrup.

Churn in an ice-cream maker according to the manufacturer's instructions. A few minutes before the ice-cream maker reaches the end of its cycle, dice the extra banana and add to the sorbet to give the mixture a little more texture. Serve immediately or store in the freezer.

MELON
SORBET

PREPARATION TIME:
10 MINUTES

COOKING TIME:
5 MINUTES

REFRIGERATION TIME:
1–2 HOURS

MAKES 1 LITRE
(35 FL OZ/4 CUPS)

BASE INGREDIENTS
170 ml (5½ fl oz/⅔ cup)
    water
600 g (1 lb 5 oz)
    Charentais melon or
    honeydew / rockmelon
    (cantaloupe) flesh
1 pinch of fine sea salt

DRY INGREDIENTS
230 g (8½ oz) caster
    (superfine) sugar
5 g (⅛ oz) sorbet
    stabiliser (optional)

Mix the sugar with the stabiliser, if using. Heat the water in a saucepan over a low heat. Add the dry ingredients in a steady stream, stiring until the sugar has dissolved.

Pour the syrup into a container and allow to cool completely in the refrigerator for 1–2 hours.

Purée the melon in a blender or food processor with the syrup and add the sea salt.

Churn in an ice-cream maker according to the manufacturer's instructions. Serve immediately or store in the freezer.

MARACUYÁ
SORBET

PREPARATION TIME:
10 MINUTES

COOKING TIME:
5 MINUTES

REFRIGERATION TIME:
1–2 HOURS

MAKES 1 LITRE
(35 FL OZ/4 CUPS)

BASE INGREDIENTS
350 ml (12 fl oz) water
400 g (14 oz) passionfruit
  juice or strained pulp
  + 2 passionfruit

DRY INGREDIENTS
250 g (9 oz) caster
  (superfine) sugar

5 g (⅛ oz) sorbet
  stabiliser (optional)

Mix the sugar with the stabiliser, if using. Heat the water in a saucepan over a low heat. Add the dry ingredients in a steady stream, stirring until the sugar has dissolved. Transfer to a container and refrigerate for 1–2 hours.

Combine the passionfruit juice or strained pulp with the syrup.

Churn in an ice-cream maker according to the manufacturer's instructions. Just before the end of the cycle, add the pulp and seeds of the two passionfruit to give a little crunch to the sorbet. Serve immediately or store in the freezer.

CLASICO SUNDAE

PREPARATION TIME:
10 MINUTES

SERVES 4

INGREDIENTS
320 ml (11 fl oz) dulce
de leche sauce
(see page 104)
320 ml (11 fl oz) chocolate
sauce (see page 104)
500 ml (17 fl oz/2 cups)
zabaglione ice cream
(see page 112)

500 ml (17 fl oz/2 cups)
dulce de leche ice
cream (see page 106)
garrapiñadas (praline
almonds, see page 144)

Spoon 2 tablespoons of dulce de leche sauce in the bottom of each of four sundae glasses. Add 2 tablespoons of chocolate sauce. Next divide half of the zabaglione ice cream between the glasses and then divide half the dulce de leche ice cream between the glasses. Repeat layers. Sprinkle with a few pralines and enjoy immediately.

DON PEDRO SUNDAE

PREPARATION TIME:
10 MINUTES

SERVES 8

INGREDIENTS

preserved cumquats, about
  50 pieces (see page 146)
1 litre (35 fl oz/4 cups)
  vanilla ice cream
  (see page 108)
2 tablespoons whisky
2 handfuls blanched
  almonds, toasted

Divide the cumquats between eight sundae glasses reserving 16 pieces. Divide scoops of ice cream between the glasses and drizzle 1 teaspoon of whisky over each. Top with the reserved cumquats and the almonds.

TRADITION

Now hard to find in Argentina, the Don Pedro sundae was traditionally made with ice cream, crushed nuts and whisky. At Clasico Argentino, we've given new life to this dish by making it with vanilla ice cream and preserved cumquats, and then sprinkling it with whisky.

CHOC-PUMPKIN ASSIETTE

PREPARATION TIME:
10 MINUTES

SERVES 4

INGREDIENTS
¼ quantity chocolate
  crumble (see page 104)
400 g (14 oz) preserved
  pumpkin in syrup (or
  other fruits in syrup)
500 ml (17 fl oz/2 cups)
  chocolate ice cream
  (see page 110)
a few small mint leaves

Divide the chocolate crumble between four dessert plates. Add a quarter of the pumpkin and a scoop of chocolate ice cream to each plate. Scatter over a few fresh mint leaves and drizzle with a little of the pumpkin syrup.

NOTES

Preserved pumpkin in syrup can be found in Argentinian food stores. If there is any left-over crumble, it can be stored in an airtight container for one week and used for other desserts or sundaes.

BANANA SPLIT

PREPARATION TIME:
15 MINUTES

SERVES 4

INGREDIENTS
500 ml (17 fl oz/2 cups)
    banana sorbet
    (see page 118)
dulce de leche sauce
    (see page 104)
chocolate chips
    and chopped
    almonds to serve

Place a quarter of the banana sorbet on each of four dessert plates. Using a piping (icing) bag with a fine nozzle or a small spoon, pipe or drizzle the dulce de leche sauce over the sorbet. Top with chocolate chips and almonds.

TRADITION

In Argentina, banana split is a traditional ice-cream flavour rather than the sundae found in the United States.

LOS DULCES

CONFECTIONERY

BISCUITS / DRINKS

DULCE DE LECHE
PRIDE OF ARGENTINA

THE TRADITION OF DULCE DE LECHE

No product in Europe has such a cult following as dulce de leche in South America. Every country produces its own version of this milk jam, with its own name: *arequipe* (Venezuela, Colombia), *bollo de leche* (Nicaragua), *manjar* (Ecuador, Chile), *manjar blanco* (Peru), *cajeta* (Mexico, where it is made with goat's milk), *doce de leite* (Brazil, also Portugal) and dulce de leche (Uruguay, Paraguay and Argentina, where it is most famous).

THE ORIGINS OF THE RECIPE

The origins of this smooth, creamy caramel-coloured spread remain unclear. It is not certain that the recipe, based on milk and sugar, was invented in South America. Even France has a claim on it—with some historians claiming that dulce de leche made its first appearance in the saucepans of a cook for Napoleon's army, who left some sweetened milk for the soldiers on the heat too long. Dulce de leche had a place in Argentinian gastronomy much earlier than this, however, since business registers from 1620 show that it was already a common import. Today, several South American countries claim the dish as their own. Indeed Argentina's claim to dulce de leche as part of its gastronomic heritage is controversial for defenders of Uruguayan cuisine. For them dulce de leche, along with the tango and the candombe, belong to the *rioplatense* heritage (shared by countries around the Río de la Plata).

HOME-MADE DDL/SHOP-BOUGHT DDL

Today, you can buy dulce de leche from shops in jars. Choose brands that are directly imported from Argentina. These are fine for biscuits and ice creams, though nothing beats home-made dulce de leche, with no preservatives and tailored to your own personal taste (more or less sweet, more or less cooked, etc). The recipe following may take a long time, but it's very easy!

TRADITIONAL DULCE DE LECHE

PREPARATION TIME:
5 MINUTES

COOKING TIME:
2.5–3 HOURS

MAKES ABOUT 1.5 KG
(3 LB 5 OZ)

INGREDIENTS

3 litres (105 fl oz/12 cups)
  milk
750 g (1 lb 10 oz) caster
  (superfine) sugar
1 vanilla bean, split and
  seeds scraped
1 teaspoon bicarbonate
  of soda (baking soda)

COOKING

In a 5 litre (175 fl oz/20 cups) cast-iron casserole or saucepan, bring the milk to a boil with the sugar and scraped vanilla bean and seeds, stirring to dissolve the sugar. Add the bicarbonate of soda and reduce heat to low. Continue cooking for 2½–3 hours, stirring with a wooden spoon from time to time. It will darken and thicken.

THE COLD PLATE TEST

To check whether the dulce de leche is ready, put a spoonful on a cold plate and tilt it. If the mixture holds its shape, remove it from the heat; if it runs a little, cook until it reaches this stage.

STORAGE

Store in an airtight jar in the refrigerator for up to 10 days.

SECRET TIP

Place a few metal forks in the bottom of the saucepan to prevent the mixture burning or the sugar catching.

DULCE DE LECHE ICE-CREAM BONBONS

 PREPARATION TIME:
20 MINUTES

 COOKING TIME:
5 MINUTES

 REFRIGERATION TIME:
MINIMUM OF 1–2 HOURS

MAKES 24 BONBONS

INGREDIENTS

350 ml (12 fl oz) dulce
  de leche ice cream
  (see page 106)
400 g (14 oz) chocolate
  (55% cocoa)

ICE-CREAM CENTRES

Fill a silicone tray of semi-circular moulds with dulce de leche ice cream or use a small ice-cream scoop and place bonbons on a lined tray. Put in the freezer. You should make 24 bonbons.

CHOCOLATE

Melt the chocolate in a heatproof bowl placed over a saucepan of simmering water. Do not let the base of the bowl touch the water.

COATING

Unmould the frozen bonbons from the silicone tray, if using, one by one. Insert a fork in a bonbon horizontally, then dip it carefully in the melted chocolate. Remove the bonbon from the mixture, tapping it on the side of the bowl. Next scrape the bonbon's flat base on the rim of the bowl. This will remove the excess chocolate and make a smoother bonbon. Using a knife, slide the bonbon off the fork onto a baking tray lined with baking paper. Repeat with the remaining bonbons. Chill in the freezer for at least 1–2 hours before serving.

MINI ALFAJORES

PREPARATION TIME:
30 MINUTES

RESTING TIME:
1 HOUR

COOKING TIME:
12–15 MINUTES

MAKES 20 ALFAJORES

DOUGH
300 g (10½ oz/2 cups)
   plain (all-purpose) flour
seeds from 1 vanilla bean
1 pinch of fine sea salt
220 ml (7½ fl oz) thin
   (pouring) cream
   (35% dairy fat)
1 tablespoon cognac

FILLING
200 g (7 oz) dulce de
   leche (see page 136,
   or ready-made)
icing (confectioners')
   sugar, for dusting

DOUGH

Combine the flour, vanilla seeds, sea salt, cream and cognac in a bowl and work together until you have a smooth ball of dough. Add a little extra flour or cream if necessary. Wrap the ball of dough in plastic wrap and rest it in the refrigerator for 1 hour.

ROLLING

Preheat the oven to 180°C (350°F/Gas 4). Sprinkle a little flour on the work surface. Roll out the dough to a thickness of 3 mm (⅛ inch). Cut out 40 circles with a 4 cm (1½ inch) cutter.

COOKING

Arrange the rounds of dough on a baking tray lined with baking paper. Bake for 12–15 minutes, or until golden. Allow to cool at room temperature on the tray.

ASSEMBLY

Spread half the cooled biscuits with the dulce de leche using a piping (icing) bag or a spoon. Place the remaining biscuits on top. Press together firmly: the dulce de leche should bulge out the sides a little. Dust each alfajor with icing sugar.

COCONUT ALFAJORES

PREPARATION TIME:
20 MINUTES

RESTING TIME:
1 HOUR

COOKING TIME:
10–12 MINUTES

MAKES 16 ALFAJORES

DOUGH
135 g (4¾ oz) unsalted
  butter, softened
100 g (3½ oz) caster
  (superfine) sugar
1 small egg
1 egg yolk
zest of ½ lime, finely grated
135 g (4¾ oz) plain
  (all-purpose) flour

200 g (7 oz) cornflour
  (cornstarch)
1 pinch of fine sea salt
1 teaspoon baking powder

FILLING
200 g (7 oz) dulce de
  leche (see page 136,
  or ready-made)

100 g (3½ oz) desiccated
  (shredded) coconut

DOUGH

In a large bowl, cream the softened butter and the sugar until pale. Mix in the egg, then the egg yolk. Add the zest. Sift the flour, cornflour, sea salt and baking powder into a separate bowl. Mix the dry ingredients into the butter mixture and bring together to make a smooth dough. Wrap the dough in plastic wrap and rest it in the refrigerator for 1 hour.

ROLLING

Preheat the oven to 170°C (325°F/Gas 3). Sprinkle a little flour on the work surface. Roll out the dough to a thickness of 5 mm (¼ inch). Cut out circles with a 5 cm (2 inch) cutter.

COOKING

Arrange the rounds of dough on a baking tray lined with baking paper. Bake for 10–12 minutes: the biscuits need to be cooked but not browned. Allow to cool at room temperature on the tray.

ASSEMBLY

Spread half the cooled biscuits with dulce de leche using a piping (icing) bag or a spoon. Place the remaining biscuits on top. Press together firmly: the dulce de leche should bulge out the sides a little. Roll the dulce de leche filling through the coconut and set aside in the refrigerator before serving.

GARRAPIÑADAS
PRALINE ALMONDS

PREPARATION TIME:
5 MINUTES

COOKING TIME:
30 MINUTES

MAKES ABOUT 1.5 KG
(3 LB 5 OZ)

INGREDIENTS
1 kg (2 lb 4 oz/6¼ cups)
  whole blanched almonds
1 kg (2 lb 4 oz) caster
  (superfine) sugar
1 litre (35 fl oz/4 cups) water

Put the almonds, sugar and water in a saucepan. Mix to combine with a wooden spoon and heat to 118°C (244°F), on a sugar thermometer, without stirring.

Take the saucepan off the heat and stir constantly until the sugar forms a 'sand' around the almonds: this is the process of crystallisation and it takes a few minutes.

When the almonds are well coated with sandy sugar, return to the heat. Keep stirring for a few minutes until a caramelised crust forms around the almonds. Stir constantly, otherwise the crystallised sugar will become a liquid caramel.

Store in an airtight container.

PRESERVED CUMQUATS

PREPARATION TIME:
10 MINUTES

COOKING TIME:
40 MINUTES

MAKES ABOUT 2 KG
(4 LB 8 OZ)

INGREDIENTS

1 kg (2 lb 4 oz) fresh
  cumquats
500 g (1 lb 2 oz) caster
  (superfine) sugar
500 ml (17 fl oz/2 cups)
  water
1 vanilla bean, split and
  seeds scraped

Wash the cumquats and remove the stems. Using a toothpick, make holes all over each cumquat.

In a heavy-based saucepan, combine the sugar, water, scraped vanilla bean and seeds and bring to the boil, stirring until the sugar has dissolved. Add the cumquats, reduce heat to low, and cover the surface of the syrup with baking paper so that the cumquats stay completely submerged, cooking for about 30 minutes.

Pour into airtight jars and store in the refrigerator.

THE TRADITION OF MATE

'MATE' IS A TRADITIONAL TEA ORIGINATING IN THE CULTURE OF THE GUARANÍ PEOPLE. TODAY IT IS MAINLY DRUNK IN ARGENTINA, CHILE, PARAGUAY, URUGUAY, BRAZIL AND BOLIVIA.

The word 'mate' (pronounced mah-tay) comes from the Quechua word *mathi*, which means a kind of gourd. This was the traditional container the tea was drunk from, through a metal tube called a *bombilla*, that also serves as a filter. The custom was to sit in a circle and pass the gourd from hand to hand, following a very precise ritual. The *mathi* is still used today for drinking mate.

The tea is made from yerba mate, a medicinal plant from South America. Its leaves, roasted and powdered, are infused in hot water. The most common method is to carefully fill the gourd three-quarters full with the herb, then add hot water. Today, you can also buy tea bags to infuse.

Drunk hot or cold (*tereré*), the tea has a strong, bitter taste and effects similar to coffee or tea. It is enjoyed for its stimulant and diuretic properties.

ICED MATE
LEMON VERBENA & CLEMENTINE

PREPARATION TIME:
10 MINUTES

COOKING TIME:
5 MINUTES

RESTING TIME:
35 MINUTES

SERVES 6

INGREDIENTS
1.5 litres (52 fl oz/6 cups)
  water
3 yerba mate tea bags
  (from an Argentinian
  or health food store)
2 clementines or
  mandarins of choice,
  cut into small pieces

2 tablespoons sugar,
  or to taste
3 sprigs lemon verbena
ice cubes

Heat the water in a saucepan and turn the heat off just before boiling point. Dip the yerba mate tea bags in the water and let them infuse for about 20 minutes. Remove the tea bags and cool.

Put the clementine, sugar and sprigs of lemon verbena in a jug. Pour over the mate tea and add some ice. Let it chill for 15 minutes in the refrigerator before enjoying.

CLERICO

PREPARATION TIME:
5 MINUTES

RESTING TIME:
30 MINUTES

SERVES 6

INGREDIENTS
3 figs
1 peach
1 banana
1 orange
1 red apple
20 red grapes
2 tablespoons caster
  (superfine) sugar

750 ml (26 fl oz/1 bottle)
  Torrontés white wine
  (see glossary)
ice cubes

Slice the figs, peach, banana, orange and apple into bite-sized pieces. Put them in a jug with the grapes, sugar and half of the wine and then gently press the juice out of the fruit with a pestle. Let it macerate in the refrigerator for 30 minutes.

Add the ice and the remaining wine. Serve as an aperitif.

ANEXOS

INDEXES

GLOSSARY

AJI MOLIDO: a widely used condiment in Argentinian cuisine, comprised of dried capsicum (pepper) flakes. Available from Argentinian grocery stores.

ALFAJOR: a sandwich biscuit filled with dulce de leche, jam or chocolate (see pages140–142).

CHIMICHURRI: a flavoursome and spicy sauce served with empanadas (see page 28).

DULCE DE BATATA: sweet potato paste.

DULCE DE LECHE: milk 'jam' that can be purchased ready-made or made at home (see pages 134–136).

DULCE DE MEMBRILLO: quince paste.

GARRAPIÑADAS: praline almonds (see page 144).

HUMITA: a traditional dish from northern Argentina, made from corn; also an edging or *repulgue* (see page 26).

MALBEC: a variety of Argentinian red wine.

MERKÉN: a widely used spice mix in Patagonia and Chile. It's a chilli powder with a strong, smoky flavour.

PORTEÑO: from Buenos Aires.

REPULGUE: the decorative edge on an empanada (see page 26).

TORRONTÉS: a typically Argentinian variety of white wine grape.

YERBA MATE: a plant used to make tea (see page 148).

ZABAGLIONE: a preparation made from egg yolks and Marsala wine.

L'ÉQUIPE CLASICO ARGENTINO

ACKNOWLEDGEMENTS

CLASICO ARGENTINO:

We would like to thank the whole team at Clasico Argentino, who work hard in the restaurants and test kitchens for the greater happiness of our customers.

A big thank you to Hélène and Morgane from the In-Mind agency for the design and layout of our restaurants: www.agence-inmind.com.

Thanks to Aymeric Albores for his collaboration on this beautiful adventure.

Our thanks go to all our suppliers, and especially Chez Antoine for his collaboration and shared happiness.

We would also like to thank Aurélie Sarrot and Pauline Labrousse.

Thanks to Florentina.

GASTON: A special thank you to Perla, Raul, Martin and Florencia for their unconditional support.

ENRIQUE: Tati and Ovi and Berna, who gave me the taste for traditional Argentinian cuisine.

INDEX

First published by Hachette Livre (Marabout) 2013
Published in 2014 by Murdoch Books, an imprint of Allen & Unwin.

Murdoch Books Australia
83 Alexander Street
Crows Nest NSW 2065
Phone: +61 (0) 2 8425 0100
Fax: +61 (0) 2 9906 2218
www.murdochbooks.com.au
info@murdochbooks.com.au

Murdoch Books UK
Erico House, 6th Floor
93–99 Upper Richmond Road
Putney, London SW15 2TG
Phone: +44 (0) 20 8785 5995
Fax: +44 (0) 20 8785 5985
www.murdochbooks.co.uk
info@murdochbooks.co.uk

For Corporate Orders & Custom Publishing contact
Noel Hammond, National Business Development Manager, Murdoch Books Australia

Publisher: Corinne Roberts
Photographer: Akiko Ida
Stylist: Sabrina Fauda-Rôle
Graphic design: Minsk Studio
Translator: Melissa McMahon
Editor: Victoria Chance
Food editor and testing: Grace Campbell
Editorial manager: Claire Grady
Production: Karen Small

Text and Design © Hachette Livre (Marabout) 2013

A cataloguing-in-publication entry is available from the catalogue of the National Library of Australia
at www.nla.gov.au.

A catalogue record for this book is available from the British Library.

Colour reproduction by Splitting Image, Clayton, Victoria.

Printed by 1010 Printing International Limited, China.

SUPPLIERS: Merci, 133 Boulevard Beaumarchais 75003 PARIS; Caravane Emporium, 22 Rue St Nicolas
75012 PARIS; Staub, 12 Boulevard de la Madeleine 75009 PARIS; Up, 14 Rue Froissart 75003 PARIS

IMPORTANT: Those who might be at risk from the effects of salmonella poisoning (the elderly,
pregnant women, young children and those suffering from immune deficiency diseases) should
consult their doctor with any concerns about eating raw eggs.

OVEN GUIDE: You may find cooking times vary depending on the oven you are using. For fan-forced
ovens, as a general rule, set the oven temperature to 20°C (35°F) lower than indicated in the recipe.